Dr. Anya writes with an honesty that is refreshing and even slightly alarming. This beautiful book is both lucid and accessible and will open doors that, whether or not the reader chooses to pass through them, will enhance their quality of being simply by being aware of them. Dr. Anya gently encourages the reader to entertain new possibilities as well as offering companionship to those who have already ventured into them. I recommend this book as an exploration of what it means to be human.
**Roshi Ingen Breen**, Soto Zen Buddhist Association

Dr. Anya's book, *Opening Love*, is a vital addition to the literature on relationships, filling the current gap that exists around relationships as a form of spiritual practice and a means of personal growth. The book presents a radical approach to relationships in comparison to current relationship books, most of which focus on a limited, and problematic, approach to achieving safety through rule-based systems. Instead Dr. Anya's focus is on relational ethics, community building and open communication: all of which seem much more likely to enable sustainable and mutual relationships.
**Dr. Meg Barker**, author of *Rewriting the Rules: An Integrative Guide to Love, Sex and Relationships*

Dr. Anya's work defuses conflict and competition to create harmony and peace. It's important that more people consider alternatives to monogamy and celibacy as ways to love more expansively. *Opening Love* comes at the right moment.
**Serena Anderlini-D'Onofrio**, PhD, author of *Gaia and the New Politics of Love: Notes for a Poly Planet*

In my life, monogamy has proved to be a less-than-perfect relationship model. I've struggled to be faithful, and I've watched friends and partners fail. When my relationships end, I ask myself why monogamy is the gold standard in our culture. I wonder if we can create other types of relationships that are more sustainable. Or at least more free, healthy and unconditionally loving? Dr. Anya says we can, and in her book, *Opening Love,* she provides a clear map for us to follow as we journey to conscious intentional relationships with many lovers. Polyamory could be a lurid, sensational topic, but Dr. Anya uses lucid definitions, a grounded rationale, practical exercises and honest accounts of personal experiences to guide us toward a life of abundant love. *Opening Love* is a brave and thought-provoking book that offers healing to those who have been wounded in the battle of the sexes.

**Marsha Scarbrough**, author of *Medicine Dance: One Woman's Healing Journey into the World of Native American Sweatlodges, Drumming Meditations and Dance Fasts*

Dr. Anya's writing comes from a place of experience and genuine desire to share what she has learned. Although she is clearly an expert and has researched her topic extensively, her approach is accessible and easy to digest. She handles the task of bringing together polyamory and spirituality with both a "how to" view as well as practical advice.

**Dan Williams**, co-host of the *Erotic Awakening Podcast* (www.eroticawakening.com)

In *Opening Love*, Dr. Anya combines her academic knowledge on polyamory, her experience as a polyamorous person, and her skills as a teacher and spiritual practitioner to present the polyamory movement's connection with spirituality. Rather than preaching about poly, this book helps the reader ask questions about their own emotional experiences and how these experiences connect with social norms and regulations. It matters not if you are monogamous or polyamorous, an atheist or a Christian: in all likelihood, you'll find something useful in these pages.

**Daniel Cardoso**, Assistant Professor of Communication Sciences and expert in polyamory studies, Lusophone University of Humanities and Technologies (Portugal)

# Opening Love:

## Intentional Relationships and the Evolution of Consciousness

# Opening Love:

## Intentional Relationships and the Evolution of Consciousness

### Dr. Anya

CHANGE
MAKERS
BOOKS

Winchester, UK
Washington, USA

First published by Changemakers Books, 2015
Changemakers Books is an imprint of John Hunt Publishing Ltd., Laurel House, Station Approach,
Alresford, Hants, SO24 9JH, UK
office1@jhpbooks.net
www.johnhuntpublishing.com
www.changemakers-books.com

For distributor details and how to order please visit the 'Ordering' section on our website.

Text copyright: Heather Trahan 2014

Author photograph: courtesy KM Keller Films
Cover image: courtesy Mandy Altimus Pond, altimuspond.com

ISBN: 978 1 78279 950 4
Library of Congress Control Number: 2014956322

A CIP catalogue record for this book is available from the British Library.

Design: Stuart Davies
www.stuartdaviesart.com

Printed and bound by CPI Group (UK) Ltd, Croydon, CR0 4YY

We operate a distinctive and ethical publishing philosophy in all
areas of our business, from our global network of authors to
production and worldwide distribution.

# CONTENTS

For Andrew:
You are the soul who awakened me.

For Robert:
Yesterday, Today, and Tomorrow.

# Acknowledgments

They say it takes a village to raise a child. The same can be said for the raising of a book. Probably the most vital energy necessary for publication is a faithful and eager reading community, offering a writer love, suggestion, question, and critique. Therefore, it is on this page I humbly express my gratitude, fully realizing that without those named below, *Opening Love* would have likely remained unopened, that proverbial dusty manuscript in the bottom desk drawer. I bow to you all. I thank you all.

The following people provided enthusiastic and wise commentary on drafts. Thank you to Meg John Barker, Frank Bartlo, Roshi Ingen Breen, Adam Brockett, Daniel Cardoso, Beth Clare Kitten Phoenix Charley, Maria Pallotta-Chiarolli, Carolyn Dalton, Laura Dawn Essenmacher, Nick Grover, Ken Hayes, Rebecca Ingalls, Amanda Itria, Caitlin Layman, Eva Lupold, Sarah Mitchell, Andrew Rihn, Carlos del Rio, Adrian Rubio, Lloyd Sparks, and Brian Streidel. Your feedback has been an invaluable gift.

Four people in particular contributed miraculous amounts of time and energy in providing commentary, as well as keen editorial advice, on significant portions of this manuscript.

To my dear loved ones Ben Murphy, Robyn Stone-Kraft, Andrew Trahan, and Robert Williams: deep oceans of gratitude! I swim in the tides of your love! Your generosity, patience, humor, and insight have allowed this book to come into being. I hope you see your beautiful selves reflected in these pages.

*Ben:* Your gentle and thoughtful critique, as well as praise, will help this book reach the right audience. Thank you for being a living model of mindfulness and courage. The simple way you live your life inspires me.

*Robyn:* You are the unexpected jewel of this project! I did not expect an intuitive, beautiful, knowledgeable writer from my early grad school days to pop up and offer insights on every single chapter. Robyn, you boldly agreed to volunteer your services before I'd even found a publisher. You live your life with a relentless and fierce passion: I hope to emulate you, as I work in the world. Thank you, Robyn.

*Andrew:* Thank you for composing the poem "An Invitation to Know What Only You Know" for the occasion of this book. There are no words that could adequately praise it. ("There are no words; you took the words!") Andrew, you are a beautiful being of light; we are lightworkers together. I hope that I have adequately conveyed the depth and sincerity of our intentional relationship, with its ups and downs and forever love, within these pages.

*Robert:* We said we shall walk through life together, and that is what we shall do. I began to write this book right around the time you began to teach me about the meaning of life. In your eyes, I remembered how the cosmos began. Our love has gently transformed me into the person I always wanted to be. Thank you for your patience. *Siempre!*

Finally, thank you offered to fellow way-showers Paul Lowe, Eckhart Tolle, and Mata Amritanandamayi (Amma). Your teachings and simple loving presence triggered the first rounds of awakening in me. Abundant peace and blessings to you, as you complete your very important work on Earth.

# Prelude

*Those who are courageous, they go headlong. They search all oppor-tunities... Their life philosophy is not that of insurance companies. Their life philosophy is that of a mountain climber, a glider, a surfer. And not only in the outside seas they surf; they surf the innermost seas. And not only on the outside they climb Alps and Himalayas; they seek inner peaks.*
—Osho[1]

It was the summer of my twenty-seventh year. My husband Andrew and I were massively in love. We rented a sunshine-yellow house, nestled at the foot of a very steep hill. We were profoundly connected. Nights, we would curl up together, snuggled like mischievous children underneath what seemed thousands of lavender blankets, reading aloud poems we'd composed for each other throughout the day.

We were magic on every level. We laughed; we played; we mused; we created; we supported; we pushed and challenged and inspired each other. And since our first date at a Chinese restaurant, three years back, we hadn't stopped talking talking talking to each other. We loved talking! Our friends playfully joked about how the two of us seemed more like girlfriends rather than husband and wife, because we were forever talking and giggling together.

In our fervor to continue this intense togetherness—to be able to keep on interacting in such passionate, energizing ways—we had agreed on one simple rule: total honesty. That was the baseline agreement. We would always tell each other the truth even if it were difficult or scary. There would be no secrets between us... or else the relationship, we knew, would end. Without honesty, without openness, there would be no Andrew and Anya. Cultivating this ethic of total honesty was what made us an especially strong couple—so much so that our friends and colleagues often called upon us for relationship advice. We were seen as a beacon of hope in a confusing world, and we relished that role. We liked helping.

It was summer. Summer, my favorite season. The season where I come alive, as always. The trees were proud in their abundant green, and honeybees drifted from flower to flower. We had known and loved each other three years, Andrew and I. We were sitting on our red couch in the yellow house we loved so much.

It seemed all saliva had dried: I kept swallowing and swallowing. It was early, just before dawn. Andrew had roused from sleep when he'd heard me come through the door. I'd just returned from spending a long—and as it turned out—quite miraculous day with Rebecca, one of my dearest friends.

I sat with Andrew, on our couch, fingers gently entwined, my whole body trembling. Armpits dripping. After a few minutes of courage-mustering silence, I said the words to him, the words I'd rehearsed in my mind all day.

"Andrew, I love you. I always will love you. And, I realize I'm in love with Rebecca, too. I love you and Rebecca."*

*Some of the people in Opening Love have retained their real names, at their request. For those who prefer anonymity, I have used pseudonyms.

# Introduction

*Definitions are vital starting points for the imagination. What we cannot imagine cannot come into being.*
—bell hooks[2]

## The Many Loves Movement

Too often, we think of "spirituality" in limited and limiting ways. The spiritual is (supposedly) what we do on the yoga mat, not what we do with our lovers in the bedroom. The spiritual is (supposedly) silent meditation, not laughing or dancing with our friends. And the spiritual heroes we idolize are often unmarried, have taken vows of celibacy, or simply seem uninterested in anything romantic or erotic. Consequently, these heroes' teachings often evade the question of sex entirely. Or, if sex does come up, it is presented in an austere or unrealistic way. For example, I have heard the Dalai Lama, on numerous occasions, teach the necessity of celibacy for those on a spiritual path.

Indeed, the term "spiritual" often evokes images of solitude: bearded gurus living alone in caves in the Himalayas, austere Catholic nuns in their tiny cells, or shamans living apart in their isolated huts. We think of Mother Teresa, working tirelessly with the nameless poor—appearing to us as an almost asexual being. We think of Nelson Mandela, imprisoned and cut off from the world for decades. Having a lover or partner often does not fit into the picture we have in our minds of who a spiritual person ought to be.

*Opening Love* questions this common view, and presents insight into how romantic love, emotional intimacy, and even our sexuality can help us grow on our spiritual path. It offers the teaching that openness to love—in all its myriad and beautiful forms—can create other openings for a life that is filled with happiness. Further, we will explore how happiness and enjoyment are not selfish states one must be overly skeptical of or shun; rather, these states are very valuable in the evolution of human consciousness.

I will forewarn: What I'm offering in *Opening Love* is not a currently popular point of view. In fact, most of my favorite spiritual teachers do not advocate what I advocate. However, the fact that this work is in print is a testament to the energy of a cultural movement that is no longer merely hiding out on the fringes but is openly and rapidly growing daily, both in the United States, Canada, the UK, and across the globe. This is the polyamory movement.

The term *polyamory* comes from a combination of both Greek and Latin roots, and it means "many loves." Polyamory (or poly, for short) is an approach to life where love is understood as abundant. People who think of themselves as poly reject the assumption that love is a finite resource. Poly people recognize love as an abundant, inexhaustible force.

The polyamory movement questions the idea that the *only* moral, ethical, or healthy way to be involved in a romantic, intimate, and/or sexual relationship is a relationship between two people. Just as the LGBTQ (lesbian, gay, bisexual, trans, queer) movement questions the assumption that the only moral, ethical, or healthy way to form a romantic relationship is to partner up with someone of the opposite sex, the polyamory movement questions the cultural assumption about number. Polyamorists ask the question: Why must we love only one?

A key tenet in the polyamory movement is the idea that it is possible to ethically and responsibly enjoy various degrees of emotional and/or physical intimacy with more than just one person. In truth, this general stance is already being adopted by many across the globe, with more and more people accepting the idea of divorce and remarriage, as well as remarriage after one partner dies. The idea of being intimate with a single mate for one's entire lifetime is increasingly becoming obsolete. The difference with polyamory is that divorce or death is not necessary to build healthy, honest connections with multiple partners. In addition, the philosophy of polyamory emphasizes that a romantic partner or intimate friendship may or may not include a sexual aspect to the relationship. Poly practitioners continually emphasize the point that sexuality does not solely define relationships.

Additionally, it is important to remember that a person can identify as polyamorous even if they do not actually *have* multiple partners at the time. For many people, simply adopting the philosophy of polyamory—where love is seen as abundant—is enough. I appreciate the way that counselor Kathy Labriola explains it in her book *Love in Abundance: A Counselor's Advice on Open Relationships:*

> Many other people embrace the theory of open relationships and enjoy having the option of having more than one lover or spouse if they should desire, but may not have the time or energy for more than one relationship, or may not have met the right person or people to enter into such an arrangement. So even though they consider themselves polyamorous, they may not "practice" polyamory—but they like having the option and having an agreement with their partner that another relationship will be acceptable if it does happen. For many people, having the freedom to choose additional relationships is as important and fulfilling as actually acting on this option and having other lovers.[3]

The polyamory movement, just like the LGBTQ movement, aims to redefine what a "relationship" is—by shifting the focus from whether or not a relationship is sexual to, instead, asking about the quality and uniqueness of each relationship. Polyamory is about letting love, honesty, compassion, and authenticity lead one's interactions. Dr. Deborah Anapol, one of the founders of the global polyamory movement, defines polyamory as a way of approaching relational life in as open and flexible a way as possible. In *Polyamory in the Twenty-First Century*, she writes:

> To me, the most important aspect of polyamory is not how many partners a person has. Rather, it is the surrendering of conditioned beliefs about the form a loving relationship should take and allowing love itself to determine the form most appropriate for all parties. If the truth is that two people freely embrace sexual exclusivity not because somebody made them do it or because they're afraid of the consequences of doing something else, I would still consider that couple polyamorous.[4]

Dr. Anapol makes a fine point here. Polyamory is ultimately not about the form—it's about the content... and if the content is about courageously following one's own desire, then that is living a life of intention, as well as a life of abundant love.

My own life is a testament to the ever-changing forms that polyamory can take. For most of my life, before I realized polyamory was even an option, I was involved a series of monogamous relationships. During the year before I wrote *Opening Love*, I was involved in a triad—a relationship between myself, my husband Andrew, and our girlfriend Katrina. That relationship was beautiful, with Katrina eventually transitioning from a girlfriend to an intimate friend. At the time I began to write *Opening Love*, I was now a member of a quad—a committed relationship of four people that included myself, Andrew, my boyfriend Mark, and Cordelia, a woman who was partnered to both Mark and Andrew. About the time I was halfway done drafting the book, I was partnered still with Andrew, and I also gained a partnership with a man named Robert while around the same time transitioning my romance with Mark to a deep, loving, spiritual friendship. Then, during the drafting of the final chapters, Andrew and I were transitioning from living together to a long-distance partnership, as he was relocating from the Midwest to the Southwest United States (along with Mark and Cordelia), in order to pursue his spiritual path, while I began preparing to move to Puerto Rico to pursue a tropical climate more conducive to my physical health. As I put the finishing touches on the book, I began living with Robert. (Please note: my use of terms such as "friendship" and "partnership" do *not* imply a hierarchy—a partnership is not necessarily superior to a friendship. The written terms used in this book are simply a reproduction of the verbal terms that I have used in my daily life that, for me, as-closely-as-possible conveys how these relationships have been mentally and emotionally organized. Because I am a human who uses language to communicate, my explanations often involve comparing and contrasting relationships, by using certain terms to describe certain people and other terms to describe other people... but, I always do it with the caveat that those terms are never precisely going to ever fully convey how much love there is, or what those people really mean to me. Language is, in my opinion, a vastly imperfect mode of communication. There are simply some things that cannot be put into words. Therefore, in *Opening Love*, when I make distinctions such as "partner" or "friend," please know I am doing my best to describe, and *not* create a hierarchy.)

Perhaps some would say that I am not a good source of relationship advice because Andrew and I no longer live together, or because my romantisexual partnerships with Katrina and Mark did not "last." I can empathize with those critiques. However, the idea that people should try to keep their relationship looking the exact same way as it did in the beginning of the relationship, as well as the idea that a relationship is successful only if it "lasts," are two very problematic ideas. These ideas are endemic in a culture that deeply fears change and denies the universal law of impermanence (more about impermanence in Chapter 3).

Every one of the people listed—Andrew, Katrina, Mark, Cordelia, and Robert—remain dear loves of mine. We trust and respect and care for each other. Therefore, none of these relationships truly ended. Nobody "broke up." Our hearts have touched, and that touching cannot be undone. Our connections will endure. The concept of *entanglement* from quantum physics is a good metaphor. *Entanglement* states that once two (or more) particles have interacted, each particle can no longer be described independently—the particles are joined, forever. The connection cannot be undone.

## Ethics of Polyamory

Of course, non-monogamy is not new. There have always been various cultures and individuals throughout history who have practiced forms of multi-partner relating, whether clandestinely or out in the open. (For a compelling as well as entertaining account of the anthropological history of human beings as an innately non-monogamous species, please read *Sex at Dawn* by Christopher Ryan and Cacilda Jethá.) What *is* new, however, is the emphasis by polyamorous practitioners that multi-partner relating be done in the spirit of honesty, compassion, and consent. No one can be persuaded or coerced into polyamory; if people are persuaded or coerced, then that relationship cannot be considered a polyamorous one. Everyone involved must freely choose polyamory.

Indeed, what makes polyamory ethical is its emphasis on consent and honesty. Polyamory is not, as some might think, merely cheating, because in polyamory all people who are involved in the situation are aware of what is happening and have negotiated specifics of the situation in a way that brings the highest possible comfort, joy, and trust.

Further, polyamory is not, as some might think, just a form of patriarchal polygamy, which is a form of multi-partner relating where a man enjoys the power of having multiple wives, with each wife restricted to intimacy/sexuality only with her one husband. Because polygamy tends to disempower women and children, the concern about how polyamory relates or does not relate to polygamy is an understandable one. However, polyamory, with its emphasis on gender equality and sexual freedom, is vastly different from patriarchal polyamory. Polyamory has its roots in feminist, matriarchal empowerment and sexual liberation movements. In the United States, for example, polyamory springs from the commune movements of the 1960s and 1970s, where equal power between the different sexes and genders was paramount.

Another misconception is that polyamory is simply another name for swinging. This is not true. While the practices are definitely related (and with some crossovers in participants), swinging is a form of ethical non-monogamy that tends to be (though not always) more about the carefree pleasures of sexual release and sexual adventure, rather than the intention to forge deep, emotional ties and/or long-term committed relationships. Also, swingers tend to be not as openly politically visible with their lifestyle, while many polyamorous people are increasingly seeking media attention, to bring polyamory to the public view.

Another aspect of the polyamory movement is the challenging of the hierarchies between different types of love. There are those in the movement who think of themselves as *relationship anarchists*. They believe that human beings should not rank relationships. For example, in mainstream society it is common to prioritize a sexual relationship over a non-sexual relationship. Relationship anarchists question this default mode of thinking.

Not all polyamorists practice non-hierarchical relating, though. Some poly people do have multiple partnerships in a way that clearly defines roles, and where everyone knows their place in the social structure. This form of poly is often referred to as the *primary/secondary model*. Here is an example of how this works. In the primary/secondary model, I might have two "primary partners"—these would be the people with whom I make a commitment to spend the most time, and to whom I pay the most attention. One of the primaries might be my legal spouse, and the other primary might be a romantic relationship that's lasted ten years. Then, I would have a few "secondary partners"—these would be the people with whom I go on dates occasionally, but they would not be as emotionally or romantically significant in my life as my primaries. It would be common knowledge to all involved that the secondary partners would not be as important to my scheduling priorities. And, ideally, the secondary partners are honest when they say they are happy with the situation. (In many cases, secondaries are not interested in pursuing a primary partnership, due to various factors such as time constraints because of a busy career or family life. Or, sometimes secondaries are healing from the wounds of a previous relationship, and for the time being, want their sexual and romantic encounters to be more light and fun than serious. )

It is also important to know that the polyamory movement is *not* a movement against monogamy, nor is its goal to destroy the institution of marriage. (Although, we as polyamorists *do* ask questions, and that simple questioning can seem very threatening from the point of view of traditional social systems.) What openly polyamorous practitioners are trying to do is to bring awareness to the fact that, for *some* people, love and sex with multiple partners is a profoundly joyful practice. Polyamorists believe there are infinite ways of experiencing love and setting up relationships. We, as poly people, simply desire to have our way of enjoying relationships be accepted (not persecuted). We also want to engage in public dialogue about love and sexuality, two topics that are often still incredibly entrenched in ignorance and dogma.

The poly movement is also bringing to light awareness that

jealousy does not have to be an automatic response to emotions, love, or sex that happens outside of the couple form. For centuries, women have been conditioned to believe that a male partner's outrage (and even violence) is a sure sign that he "really loves her." Men have been conditioned, too. Men have been conditioned that they must defend what "belongs to them." Polyamory sheds light on the reality that jealousy is *not* the result of love, but rather jealousy is the negation of love. *Jealousy signals a lack of love.* In Chapter 4, we will discuss how jealousy is not conducive to loving from a higher consciousness, and how we can begin to disentangle ourselves from that particularly devastating emotion.

Lastly, it is important for me to be clear that polyamory is not a unified movement. There are polys who practice sacred sexuality; there are polys who embrace the BDSM and kink culture; there are polys that practice polyfidelity (a closed group of partners, who are exclusive to only those in the group); there are polys who attend swinger events; there are polys who are in the closet; there are polys who embrace the "one penis policy" (a group of three or more partners with only one male in the group); there are lesbian poly groups that include only females; there are polys that practice "solo polyamory" (being single as an intentional choice); there are polys who practice celibacy; there are "unicorn hunters" (a male/female couple seeking a bisexual female); there are polys who embrace the principles of polyamory but choose not to have multiple partners. In short, there are as many ways to do poly as there are people in the world. Therefore, when I refer to the "poly movement" in *Opening Love*, please know that I am talking about a general spirit that is sweeping across the globe. This is a spirit that ponders the questions: "What is a relationship?" "What is love?"

## Confusions About Polyamory

People usually say one of two things when I tell them I am poly.

They say, "That's great, but *I* could never do that, because I'd get too jealous"… or they say, "I would love to do that, but I think my partner would want to be poly if I became poly—and I wouldn't be okay with *that*." Indeed, fear of jealousy is one of the central reasons why many who hear about poly choose not to practice it. And, at face value, that might seem like a wise choice. Why purposely open oneself to such a potentially sticky situation? Isn't allowing one's lover sexual and emotional freedom a huge risk to the relationship?

The answer to the latter question is, honestly, yes. Opening in this way *is* a risk. No doubt. By adventuring into the territory of polyamory, you agree with your partner that it is worthwhile to explore intimacy with others. However, once this journey begins, a whole host of difficult emotional states can arise, such as jealousy, anger, confusion, insecurity, and feelings of worth-lessness. Many people rightly intuit that those feelings will indeed arise if they venture into poly, and so they quickly reject the option, thus not truly seeing it as a viable option. Some people even get deeply angry that polyamory *even exists*. Once, at a restaurant, a stranger approached Andrew. The man came up close to Andrew's face, growling: *"You're* that poly guy! I hate you, and I hate what you do!"

Polyamory strikes a negative chord for many people. In the mainstream media, the discussion has gone from fear and outrage of gays and lesbians to fear and outrage of polyamorists. One of the main concerns is that polyamory appears, at surface value, to be a position that lacks stability. (Stability is a "good" that is routinely touted by politicians and community leaders.) As common wisdom has it, if one does not have the promise of exclusivity from one's partner, then surely the relationship will disintegrate in the face of competing lovers and the whirlwinds of jealousy. Therefore, if polyamory puts romantic relationships in jeopardy, then polyamory will supposedly put whole families in jeopardy, too. And without families, our nation and perhaps the whole world will crumble into chaos. Or so goes the theory.

So, why *would* a person decide to explore polyamory? Why *would* a person open to the emotional risks that polyamory usually triggers? The short answer is: This is an ideal method of transformation. To intentionally choose to face (seemingly) negative emotional states such as competition or anger or jealousy head-on is to choose to invite deep transformation, deep evolution of one's consciousness. By peeling back the layers of social conditioning that claim we must avoid these emotions at all costs, we ultimately discover that we are beings who are never actually alone, not even "alone" as a couple. We realize, paradoxically and simultaneously, our inherent unity with others as well as our inherent impermanence as human beings in a body—transformational experiences I will discuss later.

My purpose for writing this book *is not* for you to become polyamorous. I have no such persuasive goal. I applaud your choice to be whatever you are—monogamous, asexual, single, swinger, celibate monk, or something else. I write to you from a deeper motivation than persuasion. Rather, my intention is to present an offering. *Opening Love* offers the lessons I've learned from being an openly polyamorous person, suggesting how these lessons might be useful for those who are interested in living a life that deviates from the norm, and for those who are pursuing spiritual growth.

The wisdom I offer can also be applicable to those who invest their energies into deep friendships, support networks, and those connections that defy labeling or categorization. The radical insight that love is truly abundant is a message that must not be confined to just those who engage in physical intimacy and sex, but rather it's a message carrying implications for *all relationships*. Hence, while I provide some examples later in the book that focus on romantisexual relationships, I encourage you to reflect on those examples in broad ways, perceiving the core of love and care in all relationships, no matter the label or type.

## My Intention of Intention

Many poly activists understand polyamory as not just an identity or a relationship orientation. We see polyamory as a spiritual tool, as a lifelong quest for healing and wholeness. We see polyamory as an intentional way to start thinking about opening the heart, further and further, until everything that is not love and compassion is cleansed. We see polyamory as a prime example of living an intentional life.

One standard definition explains *intention* as a "plan to perform an action, which will lead to a desired outcome."[5] In this definition, we see two basic components necessary for intention: desire and action. With just the desire and no action, there is no intention. With just action and no desire, there is no intention. Intention is the fusing of these two forces—desire being the inner energetic passion, and action being the outer material/physical deed, or series of deeds. And, of course, to have intention it is necessary to use *intent*—meaning that you must, to the best of your ability, focus all (or as much as possible of) your attention on what you are trying to accomplish.

The word intention has gotten a lot of press, lately, especially from New Age authors and the emergent church movement. Thus, different definitions and approaches to the term intent/intention have begun to take shape. Internationally-renowned author Dr. Wayne W. Dyer devoted a whole book to the subject. In *The Power of Intention*, Dr. Dyer characterizes the term in a way that is reminiscent of how Taoists describe the *Tao*, a mystical, incomprehensible force that energizes all of life.

The Source, which is intention, is pure, unbounded energy vibrating so fast that it defies measurement and observation. It's invisible, without form or boundaries. So, at our Source, we are formless energy, and in that formless vibrating spiritual field of energy, intention resides... This field of intent can't be described with words, for the words emanate from the field, just as do the questions. That placeless place is intention, and it handles everything for us. It grows my fingernails, it beats my heart, it digests my food, it writes my books, and it does this for everyone and everything in the universe.[6]

Lynne McTaggart, a journalist who has a knack for distilling lessons of quantum physics for a general audience, also published a book on the subject. In *The Intention Experiment* she emphasizes the growing body of scientific evidence supporting the notion that human thoughts, desires, and emotions are not just flimsy whimsies floating around in the imaginary ether. Rather, what goes on inside our minds and hearts are an "actual physical 'something' with the astonishing power to change our world. Every thought we have is tangible energy with the power to transform. A thought is not only a thing; a thought is a thing that influences other things."[7]

As you read *Opening Love*, I invite you to reflect on what it means to live with intention. What does intention ask us to do? How does intention ask us to change? What are the prerequisites for living a life of intention? What are some of the processes and methods of being intentional? What are the outcomes of relationships backed by loving intent?

The origin of the word intention comes from the Latin *intentionem*, which means "a stretching out," involving "straining, exertion, effort." Anyone who has ever undertaken an intense exercise and nutrition regimen knows well that, first, making the choice to actively change one's physical form (as well as make the necessary adjustments to one's mental/emotional conditioning) and, then, to stick with this regimen over time is a lengthy process involving a whole hell of a lot of courage. It takes courage because mainstream culture encourages superficial changes rather than deep, long-lasting ones. This is the hidden meaning of the term. Intention as an act of courage. Intention as going against the mainstream, against the typical, against so-called "normal" thinking and behaving. (More about the concept of normal in the next chapter.)

As social science researcher Brené Brown writes in *Daring Greatly*, courage is not, actually, the absence of fear. Fear and courage are often bound up together. In fact, Brown writes, courage doesn't always feel good—it often feels like being in a "torture chamber."[8] If we perceive the link between courage and living intentionally, we prepare ourselves for the tests and challenges that will, no doubt, arise. Understanding the tension between normative cultural expectations and the courage necessary to create and maintain intentional relationships is a crucial step in emerging from the social conditioning that has falsely claimed that love is a scarce resource.

If living with intention were easy, more relationships would be harmonious. But this is not the way for a massive majority of people on our planet. I do not claim to have fully harmonious relationships (forgiveness is still a practice I am learning to cultivate), yet I *can* say that since opening my mind and heart to polyamory, where love is understood as a sharing rather than as an item to be possessed, I now rarely feel the emotion of jealousy, even though my two partners have other partners and close intimates that they love dearly. Peace, gratitude, and joy reign within my household, as well as among my network of friends and lovers. The terribly sad thing is, most people don't even know they can even hope for this kind of exuberant existence. They think that suffering and jealousy are a natural and inescapable aspect of having relationships, especially romantic ones. In these pages, I offer you another view.

To live courageously, an essential part of intention, is to move toward love. And not the Hallmark variety of love, where love is thought of as simply sexual excitement or romantic craving. In *Opening Love*, I portray love like bell hooks, the infamous feminist scholar and teacher. In one of her many books about love, she lauds the definition of love given by M. Scott Peck, in his classic *The Road Less Travelled*. Peck writes about love in a cosmic, universal sense: Love is far beyond merely romance or sex or good feelings; instead, it's about an "intention and an action" where one "extend[s] one's self for the purpose of nurturing one's own or another's spiritual growth."[9] This is the definition of love upon which this book is based. Love as spiritual growth—for both self and other.

Using this definition, it's easy to see why relationships can be so challenging. And, we can also get a glimpse into why many misguided people would wish for us to misunderstand this deeply transformative version of love... for if we began to love, *truly love*, then what would we see in the world around us? How much longer would we tolerate inequality, and even the smallest moments of violence? How much longer would we tolerate the corruption of our freedom and the planet on which we live?

As Peck writes, to love is to extend the self, *to move beyond the self*. To find connection and compassion for others. To extend oneself is no easy task; it's one that takes courage. To nurture, to give, to grow—these do not come automatically, because all of us have been conditioned to do the opposite. One must invest time, energy, and sometimes even tears.

Through peering deeply into the broken paradigm of normative relating, you will understand that the goal is not to "seek for love," but, as minister and mystic Joan Gattuso writes, the goal is instead to "find all the barriers we have built against it."[10] Courage is necessary to do such finding. It takes strain, exertion, and effort. In this current world, it often does not come easily.

As you read, you may feel annoyed with your past self, finding that you have been, either in subtle or perhaps even dramatic ways, stuck in the dogma of culture that prioritizes competition, greed, and possessiveness in not just business matters but in our intimate relationships as well. Please be patient with yourself! Knowing does not come all at once, and the evolution of consciousness is something that even the Buddha and Christ had to undergo. We begin at one place and end up at another, and then begin the journey again—this time starting from a more integrated place of wholeness. Paul Tillich, one of the most influential theologians of the twentieth century, wrote about how every soul wants to go beyond what it thinks it can do, wants to push forward to new levels of action and understanding. "Life, willing to surpass itself, is the good life, and the good life is the courageous life," he writes.[11] Indeed, to surpass is not easy. To stretch one's limits is not simple. At every turn, one will be tempted to take the easy road. However, it may be comforting to know that all human beings, by the simple virtue of being alive, are continually presented—again and again and again—with the chance to be courageous, the chance to choose a life of intention.

## Behind the Book

The journey of *Opening Love* has been a humbling process. During the first two or three years of practicing polyamory—the time during which Andrew did the heavy internal work of opening his heart to Rebecca and I began to struggle with the prospect of Andrew beginning to date other people—we often struggled. It was a tumultuous, harrowing time. We were, in the beginning, quite fearful. We kept our extra-marital relationships secret from the outside world, and we even asked our lovers to do the same. Mirroring our own insecurity and shame, our lovers often became paranoid that others would find out the truth, and they often broke off relationships with us because of that fear. For instance, my romance with Rebecca was quite brief: she ended the relationship after only a few months, nervous that her colleagues would find out. She wanted them to perceive her as straight (not bisexual or queer), as well as monogamous with her husband Paul. And even once Andrew and I mustered the courage to come out of the closet, the road was still fraught with the kind of confusions that come from living in a small town where there seemed to be no other polys with whom we could find friendship or solace.

We hope that by sharing our stories we will ease the burden of those who feel, for whatever reason, that there is something more they would like to explore, something more they would like to experience—whether that be friendships, poly relationships, non-monogamous explorations, or perhaps simply a new or renewed investment in deep, emotionally-intimate relationships that defy labels and categorization. While I am technically listed as the author of *Opening Love*, Andrew's experience and viewpoints permeate every page. He and I came into polyamory together—often stumbling, often tearful, often anxious and wondering if we were doing it right... but, always always moving in the direction of love.

## Structure and Tone of *Opening Love*

There are seven chapters. Although I have tried to roughly approximate the stages of growth necessary for understanding and practicing intentional relationships, the structure of this book is not meant to be strictly linear or follow an exact formula. Each person is different, and, thus, each will take a different path even whilst moving in the same general direction as others.

I applaud the wisdom of relationship therapist Meg John Barker, who cautions us to beware of self-help books that "promise that the author has figured it all out and is now going to provide you with answers which will enable you to have a better and happier life."[12] Indeed, no author has it all "figured out" and no book can lift the responsibility from your own shoulders about how you are going to live. You are responsible for being open to the subtle cues and clues; or, as Andrew likes to say, "It is up to you to listen to the whispers of your own heart."

As I drafted *Opening Love*, some of my readers (dedicated family, partners, friends, and colleagues) commented that my authorial voice shifts between a confident teaching voice and a reflective student voice. They offered their concern that occupying both positions within the same book—even sometimes within the same page—could be confusing for readers.

I want to acknowledge this potential difficulty. Yet, I also want to state my intention for leaving the voice shifts as they are. In many ways, yes, I am the teacher. I have authority to speak on my subject. I have written a book-length doctoral dissertation on the topic of polyamory. I have read hundreds of books on spirituality, human psychology, and the art of relationships. As a Reiki Master (a holistic health treatment), I have led seminars, workshops, and meditation sessions that have helped seekers trust their intuition. I have come out of the closet and lived for a number of years as a polyamorous person, having experienced, and consequently learned from, various circumstances as a result. I have been gossiped about; I have lost friends; I have lost financial support from my biological family; I have even been publicly ridiculed.

Yet, I am still a student. I am still learning—I will always learn. Therefore, at times I will present a concept that I am still grappling with. And, sometimes, I will present a practice that I have tested less often than some of the other practices in the book. In these moments, you will feel my student self.

I may be an "author," but I have no authority over you. I wish you freedom to consider my views and reject, accept, or modify them at your will. My intention is that *Opening Love* is a dialogue, not a lecture.

In the practices that follow, I do offer at times very specific suggestions. I offer these suggestions because they happened to work for me, and for many of my students. Yet these suggestions and the descriptions of what you might feel while you practice are just that—suggestions about what you *might* feel. In truth, you may feel none of what I describe. If that happens, please be assured, you didn't do anything wrong. Please have confidence in your abilities to try out the practice or test the idea. If you find that a practice isn't achieving the state of heart and mind that I describe, the choice is then yours of what to do next. You might find that you like the ideas in *Opening Love*, but the practices just don't sync with your personality or your schedule or some other aspect of your life. That's fine; skip over the practices. Or, you may find that the practices are helpful, but you don't agree with some of my philosophies. That's fine, too.

It is important to remember that all the practices presented in this book (or any practice you could ever decide to do) are not simply good items to be added to your life. The goodness within you is already there. The love within you is already there. The wisdom and compassion within you: already there. The practices you choose to incorporate into your daily life do not "add" goodness, wisdom, compassion, and love. Instead of thinking of these practices as additive, think of these practices as an act of pulling back and revealing. The qualities you seek through the practice are already present inside of yourself. The practices assist with engaging with what is already there.

By and large, a good way to approach this book is with flexibility and with an open mind. Be prepared to hear things you haven't heard before. And don't take it all so seriously! Have fun with the ideas, and always leave room to wonder. As you read, relax and reflect on the way your life has taken shape up to this point. If you are surprised by what I present, simply ask yourself why the surprise is there. Even if you agree with nothing I write, simply reflecting on *why* you hold the relationship values you hold can be a profound practice, as you deepen your understanding of your own consciousness.

## Notes on Language

The old-fashioned tradition of using the pronoun "he" as a way of meaning "all people" has long been criticized. However, modern updates, while awesomely carrying an implicit message of equality between the genders, can be clunky—such as using "he or she" or "she/he" or "her or his." Another possibility has been to alternate between he and she throughout the book. However, that option does not resonate with me, as I want to take into account how there are some people in this world who do *not* identify as he or she—these people may consider themselves intersex, trans, or non-binary. Therefore, when I am giving hypothetical examples about hypothetical people, my solution has been to use the inclusive term "they," a pronoun that is rapidly gaining popularity among gender and sexuality researchers.

When I use the term "partner," you can choose to view it in the typical way (meaning: spouse, husband, wife, girlfriend, boyfriend, lover, etc.), *or* you can view it as a way to describe someone with whom you have a significant connection, someone with whom you offer time, care, tenderness, and love. Therefore, a partner is a dear loved one: a person with whom you are intentionally aligning your energies.

There are suggestions for practice in each chapter. The practices vary, as I have tried to offer the methods that best facilitate intentionally analyzing or experiencing that particular theme. Some of these methods are: journaling, dialogue, bodily movement, sitting, and breathing. I hope you will experiment with these practices; my intent is that you will, for a few minutes at least, relinquish reliance on this external book and have the courage to face yourself—from the inside. These practices have been extremely useful to me in my own journey, and my students have received benefit from them also. I use the term "practice" because it's a good reminder that living an intentional, spiritual life is no different than getting really good at a hobby or a profession—it takes daily practice, which requires effort. Many people hold great philosophies about moral living, with their mouths saying how much they esteem acts of love and compassion, yet they fail to put into practice what it is they speak. Their outer and their inner lives do not match. The term "practice" reminds us that relating with intention takes practice. And delving into practice opens you up to new experiences and new trials: this requires courage.

Please remember, too, that it is easy to lose the breath during reading and study. As you explore this book, I encourage you to pause for a minute or two at the end of each section. Re-connect with your breath, feeling your body absorb the information on a different level than the intellect—through the feeling of air entering and exiting your lungs. Breathing is another way to learn.

## A True and Abundant Love

As the spiritual teacher Eckhart Tolle has written: We are at the dawn of "a new earth."[13] We, as a species, are waking up. Increasingly, we understand that people are not commodities, not possessions. A lover is not something you can "have." Loving is not a having or a holding or a getting... no. It is a free experience. A sharing.

More and more human beings are realizing the ethic of sharing as the foundation to a joyful life. Sharing support, sharing conversation, sharing ideas, sharing material goods, even sharing pleasure and sex among multiple consenting partners. This dawning emphasis on sharing is in direct conflict with the old ways—the ways of capitalism, the ways of corporate and individual greed. Sharing is *all of us* beneficially coexisting; greed is a few individuals who exploit and depress the majority. The days of greed as a standard way of doing life on planet Earth are coming to a close.

The old ways of seeing love and relationships are being revealed as not only lacking, but extremely dangerous. What we need is a sense of purpose, a sense of hope, a sense that yes we can work together to get ourselves out of the messes we have made, such as global warming, degradation of the soils and water, strife between religions and nations and races, and massive economic disparity between human beings. New paradigms for loving and living are being invented, at this very moment… and not just by spiritual teachers and poly activists, but by ordinary people who are daily doing the little things to bring sustainability and egalitarianism to this planet. Their numbers are increasing. Spiritual enlightenment is spreading like wildfire. As the mystical teacher Gangaji reminds us, "At this point in our human history, what was once reserved for the most rare beings is available to ordinary people."[14]

*You* are a part of this global awakening! *You* are a student and messenger. *You* are opening to love, to a true and abundant love, that is, absolutely, the ground of our being.

**Chapter 1**

# Dust and Dissatisfaction

*Most of us will arrive at some point in our lives when the world with which we are most familiar no longer works for us. For some people, it happens more than once. We are meant to outgrow ourselves; indeed, we can no more avoid this development than we can stop the aging process. The only question is how gracefully— and healthily—we will handle the transition. Sometimes the catalyst is an emotional or inner crisis, and sometimes it is a simple life choice that ultimately leads us in a direction we didn't antic-ipate. Inevitably, each of us will reach the moment when the place where we have felt most comfortable becomes so uncomfortable that we feel as if we are suffocating in the stale air of our own history.*
—Caroline Myss

## Slowing Down and Brushing Off

Humans are trained to let the years race by. Always one foot on the gas: faster, faster, go, go, go. Our daily lives are too often a blur of obligations and appointments, and it can be difficult to enjoy what we are doing simply because there is *so much* to do. But if we intentionally slow down, if we intentionally calm the hectic pace, what might we observe?

In *A New Earth: Awakening to Your Life's Purpose*, Eckhart Tolle writes, "The greatest achievement of humanity is not its works of art, science, or technology, but the recognition of its own dysfunction, its own madness... To recognize one's own insanity is, of course, the arising of sanity, the beginning of healing and transcendence."[15] To slow down, even briefly, reveals to us the insanity of human relating. To slow down helps us realize that we have often been unwittingly repeating a paradigm that does not bring joy, does not bring peace, does not bring love. Rather, we have been engaged in a system that keeps us isolated and afraid, always running faster, never slowing down to reflect on the depths of the potential for transformative, unconditional love. When we are slow, when we can be still, we see.

You have been handed the belief that love, sex, and relationships are a scarce commodity. You have been told to compete: to fight for what you want and fight to keep what you have. You have been handed many lies. To slow down brings presence. Awareness. Clarity. By breaking the normative fast pace, we can begin to peer behind the curtain of lies. Slowing down may involve meditation, solitary walking, quiet times of reflective journaling, a dialogue with a loved one, or anything else that removes you from the hectic pace. Slowing down gives you moments where insights have the chance to shine through.

It is likely that you have already begun to see the existence of the cultural lies surrounding relationships and the impact that those lies have had upon your life. You don't exactly need *me* to inform you of them, because your own inner knowing is strong and has already begun to speak. What I *can* offer, however, are pointers that I hope will serve as comfort for you, as well as stimulate further reflection, as you go about your journey of slowing down and brushing off the dust of cultural conditioning.

Indeed, your heart is absolutely capable of recognizing the myths inherent in cultural conditioning, all on its own. Yet, this kind of recognition often leads to confusion, despair, and a need for support. Not many people, as of yet, are asking the hard questions, and fewer still are taking active steps to change the course of their lives. Perhaps you have felt outright dissatisfaction in your relationships, or maybe what you have felt is only a slight discomfort, a vague knowing that your life isn't quite as wonderful as it could be. These feelings have prompted your initial realizations, your initial dawnings—but where do you go from there? More and more questions come. Am I alone in these feelings and thoughts? Who else has realized these truths? Why is the current paradigm of relating in place? Which of my relationships hold negative energy and how can they be transformed? What kind of relationships would bring me peace in the future? What sorts of personal characteristics must I cultivate, as I slow down and brush off? What are the next steps I might take? These are some of the questions I will address in the following chapters.

## The World of the Normal

We live in the world of the normal.

We live in a world that, for the most part, is dominated by the terror of making a social mistake. This terror is very real, and almost all of us, to some degree, worry and fret about what others may think. We base our actions on the possible reactions of others, rather than on what actions will bring us peace and joy.

Sexuality and relationships are areas, in particular, that are heavily—if not almost fully—prescribed for us by our culture. A mentor of mine, Jonathan Alexander, professor of English and expert in the rhetoric of sexuality, writes about how "narratives, stories, representations, legal codes, and ways of speaking" make certain ways of being sexual or in relationship with others seem either normal or abnormal, moral or immoral. This creates a false divide, as well as a hierarchy of options. Further, there really aren't many options at all, if one wants to avoid gossip and other forms of social censure! Teachers such as Alexander have dedicated their lives to exposing how relationships, desire, and intimacy are dominated not by our true hearts but by culture(s) that constrain us.

Much of my personal understanding has come from engaging with the work of Michael Warner, a literary critic and social theorist. Warner's ideas have been a touchstone for myself, as well as many other thinkers inside and outside of higher education for the past two decades. In one of his most popular books, *The Trouble with Normal*, he urges us to wake up to the fact that sexuality is still, in our institutions, in our public places, in our media, and in our overall culture, very confined. We may think that we are free to make choices... but, really, we are not so free. He points out that, by and large, the Western world is a very sexphobic world; we are so scared of sex that anything that hints of deviation to "normal" sexuality is scorned.[16]

*The world of the normal is a world that exists not in itself (and certainly not forever!) but only as a result of billions of people tacitly agreeing that to be normal is a good thing.* And, in this world, there is not much leeway in terms of how you can craft your life. Whether or not you consciously realize it, many of your past decisions have been based not upon your actual desires, but rather upon guessing what "they" would say: "they" being relatives, friends, neighbors, coworkers, religious leaders, politicians, and journalists. Just as you probably have, I have gotten very good over the years at guessing what they would say. It has become an almost instinctual, knee-jerk evaluation I can call up in an instant. Even now, at the times in my life when I am feeling off-balance, I still sometimes find myself sizing up a situation to figure out how much "trouble" a certain action might cost me. Even though this behavior—of weighing the pros and cons of behaving normally—is something I am actively trying to heal, I still sometimes catch myself engaging in this negative habit. Acquiring conditioning takes years, and so I remind myself that de-conditioning habitual thought patterns takes time, too. Patience is paramount. (It is a huge point of contention for philosophers whether acting in the normal way is automatically the wrong choice, or whether, with careful reflection, some actions that are considered normal might actually be the ethical or superior choice. On this point, I remain open, not wanting to draw a conclusion. Suffice it to say, however, that anything that is considered normal is, in my opinion, to be held with great suspicion and reflected upon with extra care.)

Even just two years ago, I hid under the jacket of conformity. It was winter. Andrew was unemployed; our savings account dwindling. After a number of attempts at acquiring funds had failed, I did what was, to me, a last and dreaded resort. I asked my parents to borrow money. In a series of tense e-mails and even tenser phone calls, my parents did not readily agree. Instead of offering me the money, as they had done in the past in similar situations, they questioned me on the content of what I taught in my university classrooms as well as what I was writing about in my doctoral dissertation. They asked if my academic work "promoted homosexuality." Knowing that my parents believed homosexuality a sin, I lied about my dissertation topic and I told them I never discussed sexuality in the classroom. I engaged in such lies because I predicted that being honest would mean they would not give me the money that I felt I so desperately needed. I chose money over honesty.

In the ensuing weeks, however, I felt mounting guilt, and told my parents the truth. Soon after, I began the process of forgiving them for their conditional love. However, cleansing those moments of deception did not prove to be something simple, and I am still sorting through the aftermath. If I could so easily deny my deepest ethical values, my deepest passions and drives, then what does that mean about who I am? Am I truly living a life of intention? If I wanted to seem normal to my parents, for fear that to be found otherwise would mean negative material consequences, then what kind of character do I *really* possess?

These questions have no easy answers, and they are in my mind and heart daily, as I walk through the world, now, as an openly polyamorous and queer person. (When I use the term *queer*, I mean it in the proud, reclaiming sense of the word, and *not* in the derogatory sense. More about the term queer in Chapter 2.) I have made the decision to no longer lie. I will no longer hide in the closet of any circumstance. My daily practice is to make choices without the fear of what "they" will say. I have made a solemn vow to no longer live by the norm of the normal—and this means that I will no longer engage in lying, a practice that, in many cultures around the world, is actually more accepted than telling the truth.

## Lying as a Cultural Norm

Love is blocked by the act of lying. If we do not show our true selves to others, then no real connection is possible. Therefore, telling the truth is *never optional*, whether we are speaking about why we are declining an invitation to a party or calling up our employer to tell them why we won't be at work today or telling our family that we are gay. All situations, big or small, require honesty.

In *All About Love*, the radical visionary bell hooks writes, "Commitment to knowing love can protect us by keeping us wedded to a life of truth, willing to share ourselves openly and fully in both private and public life."[17] I agree with hooks. We have been told it's okay to lie to our employer but that it's not okay to lie to our spouse. Or that it's okay to lie to our neighbor but not to our best friend. Why? We cannot pretend a lie is wrong in one sphere and acceptable in another. Dust, dissatisfaction, and entropy in relationships happen when the social pressure to conform rules us—and this conformity often calls for lies, for the mouth to deny what it knows.

That's what the world of the normal does. And, understand, it is *not* a conspiracy... it is only the result of billions of people on this planet being asleep to other ways of being. The world of the normal still seems to "work" for many simply because it sneaks in so gently, so unassumingly. It nudges, planting seemingly reassuring words in our minds: *I can hide. I can even bend a bit for them, but it won't affect my happiness. I'll be fine.*

Lying may seem a necessary evil in this world, and it may seem like something tangential to the issues of this book. But to lead lives of intention, to engage in relationships that nourish our spiritual growth, the consequences of lying can no longer be dismissed. As hooks teaches:

> Widespread cultural acceptance of lying is a primary reason many of us will never know love. It is impossible to nurture one's own or another's spiritual growth when the core of one's being and identity is shrouded in secrecy and lies. Trusting that another person always intends your good, having a core foundation of loving practice, cannot exist within the context of deception. It is this truism that makes all acts of judicious withholding major moral dilemmas. More than ever before we, as a society, need to renew a commitment to truth telling. Such a commitment is difficult when lying is deemed more acceptable than telling the truth. Lying has become so much the accepted norm that people lie even when it would be simpler to tell the truth.[18]

Our core happiness depends on whether or not we have peace in our lives. Peace is freedom from anxiety and fear. Happiness is impossible without peace. And peace depends upon whether or not we are able to be honest about the decisions we make as well as the ethical values we use to make those decisions. If we are not honest, there is always the underlying fear and anxiety that someone will find us out, or that there could have been a better choice to make.

Remember that a system of ethics is not created in isolation, but rather ethics is a term that describes how people create an honor code for working *with* others, for being a member of a community. Although each person's honor code is, ultimately, going to be different in what it contains and how it is acted out, the question of honesty versus deception is not a grey area. If we want happiness, peace, and freedom in our lives, then honesty will be the only possible choice. Granted, there will be, sometimes, certain situations where the levels of explanation needed may vary. There is no sense in being cruel. For example, when a colleague whom you find difficult asks you to collaborate on a project, simply saying, "No, thank you," may be ethically preferable to stating, "No, thank you—because I find you egotistical, controlling, loud, and obnoxious." If you simply say "No, thank you," and your colleague presses you on why you are saying no, then it may make sense to give a bit more information. This information can be done in a non-violent way, such as, "No, thank you. I think our work styles are too different to be able to effectively complete the project." An attempt to be "nice" and soften the blow by responding with, "No, thank you, I'm just too busy with these other projects," may indeed soften the blow, but it is also a lie. Such a statement makes it *seem* as though you really do want to participate, but other circumstances that are out of your control prevent you from doing so. The key, in sum, is to be honest without being unnecessarily cruel, while simultaneously not giving a false impression of your true self.

In offering a lie, you are—whether consciously or not—buying into the cultural norm of deception as a necessary part of everyday life. By lying, you participate in strengthening a broken human culture, a system where everyone feels pressured to wear a mask... and, since most of what we see of others are the masks (and not the people themselves), we don't even know how to begin to see, let alone love, each other—or ourselves. The mask becomes the reality.

∞

### Practice: Unlearning the Bends

When small children begin to speak, they do not begin with lies. They begin with truths, albeit simple truths. *Mommy, daddy, doggy, no.* They say what they see and they say what they feel.

As time passes, however, children learn about lying. They see that lying is easy; they see it is ubiquitous. Even though the adults try to teach them "lying is bad," children are smart—they see that the adults are lying every day. So the children begin to make adjustments; they begin to bend, using speech as a way to gain control over what is beginning to seem a very tenuous, strange, and even painful existence on planet Earth.

You, my dear reader, are an adult, and your schooling in the art of lying has been occurring for many years. While it is not inconceivable that your transformation to truth-telling might be rapid, it is also possible that the transformation will be an ongoing process, and that you will need to start small.

Make a commitment to yourself that you will tell the truth, no matter what arises, for one day only. Can you tell the truth all day? Just for one day?

This is where you begin the first in a series of journaling practices. I invite you to use an old-fashioned notebook and a pen (or pencil) to write. In my years as an English teacher, I have come to understand that the act of physically putting a pen to paper requires the necessary slowness that allows the brain and heart to sync together in a way that can be an excellent aid for reflection. No doubt, the computer is fine for many tasks, as it allows us to rapidly get words out of the brain and onto the screen. Writing by hand, however, is known as the mode of the poets for a reason. It is a meditative practice. Writing by hand allows us to watch the words take shape, slowly, before our eyes, in a way *that allows us to test whether or not each word is true.* Further, writing this way provokes the space and silence necessary for truth rather than lies to appear. It is easier to lie and it is easier to be careless when writing is done quickly. Just as most of us have experienced the horror of seeing a friend's rant on Facebook or some other social networking site (or perhaps we've even done it ourselves!), we can therefore understand that to take pen to paper is a process that, in requiring slowness, also requires a certain commitment.

Please be aware that my invitation is flexible, however. If you try using a notebook for a while but the practice does not seem to be activating a meditative state, please find the mode that suits you. In this practice and in others, I am sharing what has worked for me, and what I have seen work for my students—but your particular exploration may require something else. Please take what I am offering here as a basic model, tailoring the practice to your own needs and intuitions.

Open your notebook. On the top of the first page, write the words Telling the Truth Today. Draw a line down the center. On the left, write down the situations where you were presented with a choice to either lie or tell the truth. These could be big or small situations. For example, a small situation might include responding to your spouse when they ask what time you fed the cat after you have forgotten to feed the cat. It would be easy to say, "Oh, I was *just* going to do that," even though the thought was nowhere in your mind. A large situation might include having to answer your lover when they ask you whether you've just enjoyed a sexual encounter with them. It would be easy to say "wonderful," even though you were really tired and didn't orgasm.

On the right side of the paper, write down how telling the truth makes you feel, and the questions that arise during the practice. It would be best to pull out the paper and add to it throughout the day, and not wait until the end of the day to try to remember—because it is likely that, by waiting, you will have forgotten most of the details.

As you fill in the left column, you may find that you are unsure about the level of description that should accompany telling the truth. Write down your confusions and any questions that you have, for later reflection. Be prepared to note any occasions where you fell short of telling the truth, or situations where you told only a partial truth. These are the bends, the situations where you succumbed to the false voice of cultural conditioning, the voice that assured you that a little bend would do no harm.

At the end of the day, analyze the list as a whole. Note if any patterns emerged. Flip the page, and on the backside, write a few paragraphs in response to the following questions:

Was it more difficult to tell the truth to one person or a group of people in particular?

Was it difficult to tell the truth about emotions, relationships, finances, daily routines, personal needs/wants, or intellectual ideas? Did you lie or want to lie as a way to appear "normal"?

If you did not tell the truth in certain instances, what about those particular situations triggered fear? What was the root of the fear hiding underneath the lie? Does this fear deal with feeling physically, materially, or emotionally vulnerable? How often do you feel this type of fear? In what relationships do you feel the consistent need to lie, because this fear is overwhelming?

This journaling practice is meant to help you see more clearly the patterns of your heart. If you can be honest with yourself, first, about the existence of lying in your life, then you will be on the road to transforming your relationships. In so doing, you will effectively extract yourself from the toxicity of "normal" life—the normality of lying.

As you complete this practice, it is important that you carefully balance the act of recognizing your lying with the emotion of love and compassion directed toward yourself. Love yourself! *Love yourself even when you catch yourself in a lie.* Yes, you may be momentarily frustrated by your actions or confused about why you engaged in the lie, but—as quickly as you can—come back to a feeling of love for yourself. We can be experts at condemning ourselves. Be open to what you see about yourself without being harsh. Know that you are being courageous by doing this internal work. Whatever happens as a part of the process is wonderful. Ultimately, even though lying is an action that you no longer want to participate in, do not label lying as "bad" or "wrong"—because labeling in this way inherently involves self-judgment. And, if you self-judge, you may feel more comfortable labeling others as bad or wrong—which causes disconnection, separation, and negative emotions. (We will discuss the pitfalls of labels further in Chapter 3.)

Ultimately, the goal of this journaling practice is to uncover the normality of lying in yourself… and, then, as you live in a new way, others will see the changes in you and begin to look within, just as you have done.

## Expectations

In the world of the normal, there are assumptions and expectations. There are benchmarks all of us are supposed to reach. In the current paradigm of relating, the goal is to be normal—or, at the very least, *appear* normal. In many parts of the world, what we do in romantic relationships has been carefully prescribed for us. It is considered normal, and thus ideal, to:

- Stop having sex and stop having intense physical contact with other people after saying "I love you" to your partner.
- Move in together after an appropriate amount of time has passed.
- Get legally married, or have a public commitment ceremony.
- Acquire a house and other material goods.
- Raise children.
- Stay together until death, or get divorced.

Not only are we pressured to hit those benchmarks in that specific order, we are supposed to hit them within certain age ranges and with certain types of people. We must also express certain emotional values, and take part in certain activities. There is so much we are supposed to do, so much we are supposed to say and be.

The sexuality theorist Eve Kosofsky Sedgwick often mused on

the utter ridiculousness of *normativity*, a term meaning the collective social pressure to be or seem normal. Much of her writing was about families, exposing the myriad hidden cultural expectations and prescriptions. In her book *Tendencies*, she showed how the simple concept of "the family" is not so simple, because it holds within itself a set of unrealistic expectations. For example:

- all members of a family must bear the same last name
- a family must have a romantic couple at its center
- a family must be a legal unit
- a family must be centered in a building/home
- a family must produce and care for children
- a family must accumulate material goods and pass them on to successive generations
- a family must have a daily routine and a regular schedule
- a family must be a site of patriotism[19]

To gaze upon such a list is to realize that no family can ever truly conform to all that culture expects of it. Granted, the push to be normal is not so obvious as it was in the 1950s or earlier eras. And even the way we are conditioned to love is not as rigid as it has been in the past. As William J. Doherty points out in *The Intentional Family*, up until just a handful of decades ago, people were required to choose a marriage partner based on kinship obligations: a spouse was supposed to be someone who would bring honor or wealth to one's biological tribe.[20] In today's culture, however, one marries for reasons of love and passion… thus, gazing today versus yesterday seems to belie a certain freedom of choice. One can marry whom one wishes, at least hypothetically.

Yet, this supposed freedom is veiled under a thick layer of dust. The current paradigm is not a paradigm of freedom at all.

∞

## Practice: Finding the Rhythms

Take a walk out in the natural world. Find a beach, stream, park, trail, path up a hill or mountain. Hear the sounds, smell the smells, and see the sights. Immerse yourself in your senses. Touch the bark of a tree and feel what that feels like under your fingertips. Is it hard or soft? Cool or warm? Bring your nose to the tree. What does that smell like? Sit down and spend a few minutes with a flower. Do not pick the flower, but allow it to continue its home in the soil, appreciating it for what it is—a burst of colorful magic.

Devote at least an hour to this practice. As you begin to loosen, as your mind begins to soften, allow yourself to intuitively absorb and reflect upon the natural cycles around you. What season is this? What life forms here are fresh, young? What life forms are decaying, dying? What life forms seem to be cresting at full vibrancy? What animals are grouped together? What animals appear to be alone? What activities are the animals engaged in? Can you sense any emotions from the animals or plants?

One thing that is certain is this: Intentional relationships must begin with an *internal* intentional relationship. One of the best ways I have found for brushing off the dust and digging deep into who and what "I" really am is to unplug and explore my deepest home—not my apartment and not my city, but Planet Earth.

Spending time in the natural world can be an exquisitely simple yet demanding teacher, who helps us understand what is most basic, what is inalterable in terms of rhythms and cycles. In the Taoist tradition, it is advised to spend at least a few minutes, every day, away from the social world of work, technology, appointments, buildings, cars, roads, clocks, and other people. The natural world, for Taoists, is crucial for recharging one's life energy: what they call *Ch'i.*

Human beings have created an extraordinarily stressful blueprint for how life "should" go. People "should" get married and people "should" have children and they "should" do this and that in order to be normal. These should's loom over our lives and cause anxiety, in both conscious and subconscious ways. Spending time in the natural world and observing what is necessary for animals, plants, and other living beings helps us to put into perspective what we *really* should do in order to live in a state of abundant joy, and what activities or pursuits can be pruned. In many ways, the garden of life is simple... while humans, with their social rules and lengthy lists of expectations, make life (appear) difficult.

What are the expectations, requirements, and benchmarks others have set for you? Which of these do you feel are exciting possibilities, and which feel like constrictions or burdens? By spending time in the natural world, you will begin to understand the distinction between the activities that human beings really need to do versus the activities that are merely social pressure. By recognizing that distinction, you are better equipped to make choices that bring you peace, rather than stress and suffering.

## A Broken System

When I hold workshops and discussion groups on polyamory, one of the truisms my participants frequently mention is that monogamy is a necessary social force—one that glues families together, and also brings people the maximum amount of happiness. Yet, the statistics tell another story. With around half of marriages ending in divorce, up to two thirds of married couples having affairs, and one in three people living alone,[21] it would be strange *not* to ask: What's going on here? Why do people become unhappy with their partner as time passes? Why is deception so rampant in relationships? Why is it so difficult to find and cultivate a joyous union with a loving companion?

The situation with monogamous marriage is just one example

of the disconnect between what people say they want versus the reality of what people do. The chasm is wide. Many people pay lip service to the awesomeness of monogamy, and yet they cheat or have secret fantasies. Many people make lifelong marriage vows, yet they divorce, ditching their old partner for a shiny new one as soon as the sex gets stale or the deeper problems become apparent. Many people swear they want love, yet they are not willing to always tell the truth to their partners or friends, and live behind a wall of secrecy. Many tout freedom as the ultimate good, while subtly trying to manipulate their partner.

From whence does this insanity arise? Maybe it is not so much a matter of people having a lack of intention or being lazy with their lives, but rather, maybe the problem stems from being asleep to the questions: the questions that then get people *started* on their path of intention. People rush around ("time is money") taking the common wisdom at face value, without slowing down to ask whether or not this common wisdom has actually brought happiness.

Caroline Myss has written and lectured extensively about the concept of what she calls "tribal consciousness." According to Myss, tribalism is a way of life where the norms and expectations of one's biological family, as well as the larger communities and cultures that have birthed that particular family, are given dominance in an individual's life. In fact, obeying the tribe means that there really is no individual at all; there is only a bee in a swarm of other bees, dutifully carrying out the queen bee's (culture's) dictates. Myss asserts that although the twenty-first century has indeed come, a remarkable majority of people still submit their will, sacrifice their passions, and silence their conscience to the norms of the tribe.

In essence, "the tribe" is a shorthand way of talking about the complex intersection of various tribes that try to influence one's life. Indeed, it is important to understand that there is never just one tribe, but there are many, and they all have various areas of rule and reigns of power.

You don't have to look to foreign lands to notice this behavior. Flip on the evening news or look out your window. The tribe preaches that their country is the best, and so men sign up for military service and find themselves committing atrocities. The tribe dictates that more money is good, so business owners lower their employees' wages while pocketing the balance. The tribe dictates the idea that some people are just born lazy, so politicians cut funding for assisting those in need. The tribe dictates that humans are the most important beings on Earth, and so every night millions of people sit down to dinner, consuming the bodies of animals who have been tortured from the first day to the very last day of their lives. The tribe dictates that a thin frame and large breasts are what is desirable to a heterosexual male, so young men go to bars, scanning for potential lovers, eventually going to bed with women who fit the criteria, regardless of whether or not there is a loving connection between them. The tribe dictates that financial stability is the all-important good, so many people marry, even though they do not feel passion. The tribe dictates that the bodily pleasures are suspect, and so people in restaurants lower their voices when they speak words like "sex" and "orgasm."

The tribal elders—parents, teachers, political and religious leaders—tell us how to live our daily lives in both subtle and obvious ways, from the small matters such as whether we should dye our hair or get a tattoo, to the large matters such as what neighborhood we can live in and who we should marry.

Here is an example. There is a little girl, about five or six years old. At school, she befriends another little girl. The two girls have a wonderful time at school. They giggle in the hallways; they eat lunch together. Eventually, the little girls ask their mothers if they can play together after school, and their mothers agree. So, they visit each other's homes. The girls have a wonderful time, just as they did in school. When the mothers occasionally peer in at them, quietly opening the bedroom door, they often notice the little girls beaming, laying on the bed, holding hands, stroking each other's hair or tickling each other. The mothers love to see these interactions—they see it, and know their daughters are happy. One day, one of the little girls befriends a boy at school. The little girl and the little boy feel very happy around each other: They like to play, tell secrets, and share. The little girl's feelings are no different than the feelings she has for her female friend. The bond is wonderful! One day at school during recess, the little girl and the little boy are playing a game of chase. The girl catches up to the boy, and she wraps her arms around him. She gives him a big kiss—she loves him so! The teacher sees this behavior. She scolds them. She says, "Boys and girls do not kiss at school." The children are confused, particularly the little girl— because in the past she had kissed her female friend in plain view of her teacher, and her teacher had said nothing.

When the teacher scolds, she does not realize she is training her students about tribal notions of gender. She is training them about how girls and boys, men and women, are supposed to behave. She is training them about sexuality, love, and friendship. She is training them, in this single act of scolding, perhaps hundreds of subtle lessons about what is "normal" and what is not.

Even though this training by the teacher is potent, other tribal leaders will need to reinforce the lessons. A few months later, the little girl asks her mother if her good friend, the boy, can come over and play. The mother agrees, but warns that the little boy must not play in the little girl's room. The little girl is confused. "Why not?" she asks. The mother says to her daughter, "Little boys are very different from little girls, and it would not be proper." With this information, the mother further engrains countless norms, norms that the teacher had begun to teach: norms about heteronormatity (that the normal way to be is to be romantically/sexually attracted to the "opposite" sex), norms about gender disparity (that there is a war between the sexes); norms about sensuality (that sensuality always leads to acts of sexuality), and more. The teacher and the mother have begun the process of tribal conditioning, and the little girl will absorb these bits of tribal wisdom from other people as she continues into adulthood.

It is important to understand that people are *not* stupid or lazy for following these group belief patterns. Humans are conditioned from day one of their Earthly existence. Countless lessons are imprinted, from the very first moments of life outside the womb. Today, a majority of babies in developed nations are born in hospitals, where they are taken from their loving mother seconds after the delivery, and are whisked away to a cold, sterile examination area with bright lights and bright sounds and medical devices that are jarring for a delicate newborn who has just spent the previous nine months in a warm, dark, soft, peaceful womb. After the baby is poked and prodded, they are then taken to a tiny box in a nursery, separated from their mother for many hours. They wonder: What *is* this horrible, hostile place? Why am I alone? Where is the warmth of my mother? The answers to some of these frightening questions become some of the core lessons instilled by the Tribe, albeit unwittingly. These lessons are imprinted deeply, and they have consequences for adult life.

There is, however, a surprising twist to this depressing story of conditioning. *The ultimate purpose of the tribe is never to harm, but to try to keep you safe.* This is an important point to remember. The tribe is never, at core, sinister. It cannot be boiled down to an evil conspiracy. It never *knowingly* misleads people or brings them harm. The tribe is merely an *unconscious collective* trying to do good for the whole by keeping individuality at bay. Therefore, it is not necessary or productive to direct anger at the tribe. It is only necessary to forgive. (I will share more about forgiveness in Chapter 6.)

We all wake to our own power through a number of mechanisms. Some of us acquire an illness and are therefore forced to reflect upon our lives, asking what needs to be transformed in order for healing to take place. Some of us wade through a deep, halting depression, until we hit the bottom so hard that we must choose either darkness or light, death or life. Some of us age, and in the process of losing what the normal world calls "beauty," we realize we care more about radiating the growing love inside our hearts.

While the process is always unique to each person, what is not unique is the fact that some growing pains are required when the world as you know it unravels. You have begun to realize what you thought was your freedom was not. The next part of the journey will have you ask questions like: So, what's *underneath* the dust of cultural conditioning, and how do I retrieve it? What is my desire?

# Chapter 2

# Queering Desire

*It is said that—*
*enlightenment appears dark,*
*the progressive way appears retrograde,*
*the smooth way appears jagged,*
*the highest peak of revelation appears empty like a valley,*
*the cleanest appears to be soiled,*
*the greatest abundance appears insufficient,*
*the most enduring inner strength appears like weakness,*
*and creativity appears imitative.*
—Tao Te Ching[22]

## The Old Way and the New Way

For thousands of years, there have been innumerable teachings on the subject of desire. In some Buddhist traditions, for example, desire and suffering go hand-in-hand. Desire is seen as the ultimate symptom of dissatisfaction (*dukkha*), keeping human beings stuck in negative thought patterns and destructive egoic actions.

Teachings about the dangers of desire have made sense for thousands of years, helping countless people achieve more peaceful, more free and awake lives. However, this bleak definition of desire is beginning to pass away in the collective human consciousness. What replaces the old definition is the concept of desire as a foundation for an intentional life, and a trigger for the courage necessary to live such a life.

Spiritual teachers are starting to teach desire differently. The message is spreading that spirituality is lifeless if it does not embrace feelings, sensuality, and desires. Instead of automatically mistrusting desire, we can view it as a potential energy of connection, one that is in fact necessary for living a passionate, intentional life. In truth, this new way of viewing desire is not new at all—it is a revitalization of the practices and beliefs of Native American and other Earth-based indigenous peoples, as well as pre-Christian matriarchal cultures. These ancient world-views understood sexuality, sensuality, emotions, eroticism and relationships as inextricably entwined with a spiritual path.

It must be noted, however, that there is a difference between craving reckless and empty pleasures versus desire for the joy of intentional relationships. There is indeed a fine line separating the two, and the art of discernment is necessary. Unfortunately, the wisdom needed for such discernment is not valued in current normative mainstream culture. Such wisdom is not taught in schools nor is it taught within most families.

Wisdom is necessary for understanding where to stand when you are faced with that fine line... what is desire, and what is not? In this chapter, we will begin to consider desire from a new angle, a queer-er angle. We will see how desire is integral to charting out a new path for intentional relationships.

## The Voice of Desire

Have you ever heard a strong clear voice come into your mind? You may have been sunk deep into meditation, or maybe you were on the verge of waking from sleep. Perhaps you were simply going about your daily life, completing some mundane task.

This voice took you by surprise. When it spoke, it seemed to take an incoherent feeling and perfectly shape it into language. Hearing this voice was both a shock and a relief. The voice (you noticed it sounded somewhat like your voice, but it wasn't exactly your voice) gave you a blatant command or an idea of what direction to next take in your life. When you heard the voice, you felt a calm certainty in your gut and a wave of love wash over your being. You felt, during those moments, a complete absence of doubt. This is the voice of desire.

Desire is your inner wisdom; it is your intuition; *it is what you, at your core, truly are.* If you listen to this voice, and courageously act upon its callings — even if it is difficult, even if it strains you — then you will be living a life of intention. You will change and every single one of your relationships will change.

However, interpreting that which is the voice of desire can be enormously challenging, especially for people at the stage of life where they are just coming to realize the importance of slowing down and listening. The difficulty of the situation, as explained by shaman Don Miguel Ruiz in *The Four Agreements: A Practical Guide to Personal Freedom*, is that there are other voices swirling around inside of us, too.[23] These other voices sometimes speak up, in a similar fashion, and thus they compete with the voice of desire. So, we become confused. We become cynical or dismayed or depressed. We spin and spin, not moving forward, not taking action, not wanting to make a mistake, hesitating. We lose faith in ourselves.

## To Queer Desire

The term *queer* used to be an insult. Now, in academic communities and in many progressive places across the globe, the term *queer* is taking on new, positive meanings. As a noun, it is being used to celebrate a non-heterosexual identity. To be queer is to be courageous! To be queer is to be sexually liberated! Additionally, the term is also being used as a verb. This new verb, queer, means an action, a movement, a shift or a change. To queer something is to productively turn a concept or a situation on its head in order to view it from a new angle.

To queer something helps us observe a phenomenon in a new way and produce new insights. We can queer anything. A teacher can queer a classroom by asking students to sit on the floor instead of in desks. By doing so, the teacher can then analyze how this disruption of the traditional way of doing things (desks) has impacted how students learn. A Reiki practitioner can queer traditional modes of healing by placing their feet, rather than their hands, on a patient.

To queer is to experiment. To queer is to try something new, usually in ways that break tradition. To queer desire is to turn desire over, and inspect it from a new view.

## No More Normal

To talk of life as enjoyment and happiness seems an impossible dream to many people. It seems naïve. They do not see how it can actually happen. Not only that, but also many religions categorize enjoyment and happiness not as states to aspire to, but as states to actively avoid—because one must supposedly wait for an afterlife.

Suppose a friend asks you, "What are your life goals?" If you reply, "To be happy; to enjoy life," that person is likely to squint at you either in confusion, disbelief, or mockery. To feel happy? To enjoy? That's all?

Your friend is likely confused because the normative response to the question "What are your life goals?" is to fill in the blank with all the specific professional and personal goals that one wants to achieve, as well as the rewards one wants to claim. Some typical answers are: to own a home, to have a child, to become president of a company, to stay married for a lifetime, to retire to the tropics, to make a million dollars. The simple response you gave your friend—to feel happy, to feel enjoyment—is vastly different from these normative responses. So your friend's mind temporarily short-circuits. They do not understand what you mean. They may even wonder if you are naïve, stupid, or maybe even a bit crazy.

This is the path you must walk if you choose a life of intention. You must be content with others viewing you in a less-than-favorable light. You must be content with appearing as your true self, as someone who does not strive to be normal, who does not dream of the crowd. To follow the voice of desire, you will enter a doorway to a kind of living where you see that happiness and enjoyment, far from being secondary benefits, are actually core components of an intentional life.

## Sensitivity and Desire

When that strong clear voice of desire speaks within, it is necessary to be in tune with the whole situation. As I mentioned earlier, there are other voices that compete for your allegiance. What to do?

Your voice of desire will guide you toward what you need to know and what you need to do next. Yet, how do you know which is the voice of desire and which are false voices, voices that arise from false dreams? In order to answer this question, it is necessary to understand the link between sensitivity and desire.

As you become more aware of the competing voices, you will need to become even more sensitive than you already are. In the English language, it is true, however, that the word "sensitive" has gotten a bad rap: being sensitive is often seen as weak or naïve. Just as spiritual teachers are reclaiming desire as a positive aspect to life, many are also reclaiming sensitivity as a positive trait.

Being sensitive is being able to sense. To sense is the basis of all wisdom. If we do not sense something, it is not there; it does not exist. Therefore, cultivating sensitivity is a helpful attribute, one that is crucial for evolving one's consciousness.

Everyone is born with a certain amount of sensitivity, with the ability to perceive both the material (what you can touch, taste, see, hear, and smell) as well as the non-material, which is everything else. Infants and young children are still very much in tune with the non-material—consequently, this is one reason why adults love to be around infants. They are shining little creatures of light, in touch with all forms of entities and energies that our adult logical brains and our cultural conditioning have told us are false or imaginary. As children get older and enter school, they are indoctrinated into the so-called normal world—a process that has the unintended (or perhaps sometimes intended) outcome of squelching sensitivities to the non-material world.

Let us return to the example from the first chapter. The little girl adores her friend the boy, and she senses that if she stays close to him that they will have so much fun together. She instinctively senses the deep circuits of energy that draw her to him and he to her. When she touches his hand, she feels a tingle in her spine; when he is laughing with her, she feels her crown fill with a warm, soft vibration. But the little girl then learns from her teacher and mother that what she senses is inappropriate. She learns that the energy she feels for the boy is dangerous and suspect. She learns to fear not only that particular boy but also all males, while also paradoxically learning to seek their sexual adoration (rather than the sexual adoration of females). Over time, she loses touch with all ability to sense the non-material energy that emanates between people when they have a strong connection.

*Every single human being you know has undergone this harsh process of cultural conditioning.* Even the Buddha underwent this process. He began life as a prince named Siddhartha. His royal tribe taught him that what mattered in life were shallow pleasures: the pleasures of food, drink, material objects, and sex in ways disconnected from any deeper significance. Paradoxically, Siddhartha was taught that happiness and enjoyment were the supreme aims—and yet he was not given the necessary spiritual knowledge for actually attaining that happiness and enjoyment.

Experiencing happiness and enjoyment on a daily basis is the process of awakening. Some call it evolution or spiritual enlightenment. Others call it wisdom or understanding. It matters less what word you use, and more that the word you select resonates with your heart.

In the process of awakening, the link between desire and sensitivity becomes clear. Osho, one of the most compelling spiritual teachers of the twentieth century, reminds us that many people are not yet able to perceive what their desires are, because they have become dull with fear and monotony. Their tribe has taught them that risk is dangerous, that a life of safety and predictability is a good life. In *Courage: The Joy of Living Dangerously*, he writes:

> Existence goes on showering on you, but you are enclosed in your past. You are almost in a kind of grave. You have become insensitive. Because of your cowardliness you have lost your sensitivity. To be sensitive the new will be felt—and the thrill of the new, and the passion for the new and the adventure will arise and you will start moving into the unknown, not knowing where you are going.[24]

Indeed, many people cannot feel, cannot perceive the call of "the new," the call of "adventure." They are trapped in their fear and they do not know how to be courageous. Their lives are nearly motionless, their sensitivities dulled. The voice of desire may arise within them from time to time, but it is ignored, either due to sheer fear or perhaps because of the confusion due to other competing voices.

To live a life of intention is synonymous with living a life of enjoyment and happiness. And the angel leading you to this heaven—ever present, ever at your service—is the voice of desire. Difficulties may arise, confusions may arise, even sorrows may arise... but those states are all temporary, and you will relax into them, because you will perceive them as temporary. Seeing the transitory nature of these mental/emotional states will free you from fearing them. Freedom from fear is the ground upon which you can embrace the voice of desire and discard the other voices, the voices born out of tribal conditionings.

∞

## Practice: Uncovering Tribal Lessons

Have you ever noticed how it can be so easy to give advice to friends in difficult situations, but when you yourself are undergoing a similar situation, you can feel so lost, so unsure? Often, it is easier to look at a situation both analytically and intuitively if the situation belongs to someone else. In this practice, you will use the situation of someone else (Anya) as a way to tap into some of the deep tribal conditionings that hold fairly common across many walks of life. For example, the tribal lesson of heteronormativity (the lesson that romantic relationships must be between a "man" and a "woman") runs rampant across both the Midwest and the Northeast and the Southwest and all other regions across the United States. There are many tribal lessons like this that work at the macro level, encompassing many regions, races, ages, genders, and socio-economic statuses.

Re-read the Prelude. Put yourself in my shoes. If you had been deeply in love with your spouse, yet you realized you were also simultaneously in love with your friend, what sorts of conditioned tribal lessons would this realization bump up against? Take out your notebook and list as many of these lessons as you can. Aim for listing at least a dozen. Be as specific as possible. As an example, you could write down the tribal lesson that romantic love is diluted if your desires stray from your partner.

After listing as many tribal lessons as you can, take some time to meditate. Focus on your breathing and thus tap into your intuition. Expand your belly on the inhale for seven seconds, hold the breath for seven seconds, and then exhale while contracting your belly for another seven seconds. Repeat this cycle a number of times. Notice calmness wash over you. Be completely in the moment, with just the sound and feeling of your breath. In this way, you will absorb the insights from the journaling on a different level. You will be sensing your insights, but not from logic, not from your mind. You will be storing these insights within your new sensitivity: your desire.

## Desire as a Living Being

Desire is a being. It is alive. It is a part of you, and it is also part of the whole.

Because desire is alive, it is important to see how we can sense it and work with it in symbiotic ways.

Jesus once said, "If you bring forth what is within you, what you bring forth will save you. If you do not bring forth what is within you, what you do not bring forth will destroy you."[25] One interpretation of this teaching is that Jesus was talking about desire. This voice of inner knowing speaks to us loudly and clearly. It points us in the direction we need to go, the direction that will bring about the most enjoyment and happiness. It is a gift of life; it simply is available to us *because* we are alive, *because* we are here. To "bring forth" desire is to notice it, ponder it, value it, and then use it as fuel for intentional action—and, most certainly, that action will require tremendous courage, because the way of the world (at least for now, at the time I write this book) is a way that does not honor desire. The way of the normal world is a way that honors fear. Therefore, to go the way of desire is to go the contrary way, the way of the rebels.

If we bring forth desire, if we bring forth what is naturally within us, we will be saved—and not "saved" as in some sort of afterlife, but, rather, saved *now*. *Saved in this lifetime.* We will be saved from a life of fear and anxiety. We will be saved from the normative doom that is the reality of so many lives: Lives where employees do not quit when they are faced with joy-killing conditions because they fear not being able to find work that makes them happy; lives where wives do not leave husbands who abuse them because they feel they do not deserve a loving relationship; lives where people drag themselves out of bed and feel they need to slam cups of coffee in order to face the day. For so many, life has been stripped dry. There is nothing to discover and there is nothing new to know.

There are, of course, levels of awareness. Some people know that a better life is possible, and so they take courageous steps, while still falling short of a fully joyous life. Here is an illustration. My dear partner, Robert, was working at a car factory. After having been required to work fifteen consecutive days, he was informed by his boss that there would be no more weekends off until further notice. Upon hearing this mandate, Robert quit. Despite the lack of jobs in our geographic area and despite the fact that he had no savings, he would not be exploited in this way. He knew he could no longer work for those who treated him with a complete lack of empathy. He knew that adequate time to rest his body and mind was not mere luxury, but rather a necessity for the kind of life he wanted. Weeks later, Robert found work at another factory. Yet the new job was so similar to the one he had left. While he was always given weekends off to rest, which was indeed wonderful, he was paid even less. He therefore struggled to pay his bills, even though he worked very hard for the company.

Robert is an astounding man. A holy man. He heals; he counsels; he listens; he gives of himself so generously. I have seen him transform lives. His energy is so loving, so patient, so pure and clear that he heals people by merely sitting next to them. Helping others is effortless for him: it is what he does naturally, by simply being himself.

So I wonder: Why is this amazing man stuck in a cycle of low-paying, low-respect jobs? Why does he give so many hours of each weekday to those who do not pay him decent wages, a situation that causes him a fair amount of anxiety and frustration? Why does he not trust that, despite only having a high school diploma, there could be a better path for him, a creative way to make an income that would fulfill his true desires, his true self? When he quit the car parts factory, he trusted, perhaps against logic and reason, that better employment was possible. He knew he was a valuable human being and did not deserve to be exploited, so he took the courageous step of quitting a job even though he had no backup plans or safety net. Yet, it has become clear to me that working these types of low-respect, low-paying jobs has always been one of the most difficult aspects of his life. Some days, yes, he can achieve a Zen-like state whilst at work: he can tune into the magic and mystery of life and even bring joy to his coworkers. But, as a whole, he does not intrinsically love the work. It is not his desire.

There are, of course, levels of awareness. There are people like Robert: a person at the level of knowing that better is possible and courage is necessary. There are others, on the other hand, who are so unconscious that they are quite unaware that there is even an alternative to the norm. For example, on the last day of work at the car factory, he overheard his coworkers muttering "oh well, we gotta do what we gotta do," and "not much we can do about it" in response to the news that they no longer would have weekends off. Those people, while perhaps aware of being exploited, were not aware that they had the power to transform the situation. What did they feel as they watched Robert walk away? Did they feel terror for him, or envy? Did they think him naïve? Robert was (to his knowledge) the only one who quit that day. The others succumbed to the fear, the fear that without this job they would lose their families, their houses, their cars, etc. They were stuck in inaction, unable to exert the courage necessary to follow the voice of desire.

Jesus warned about failing to bring forth desire. To *not* bring forth desire is to let desire stagnate, and eventually poison. In a life where desire is repeatedly ignored, that desire begins to rot, fermenting inside of us and causing a toxic sludge. The very cells of our being become coated with this poison. Our cells can no longer communicate with each other, and it becomes very difficult to discern what to do in daily life. This miscommunication affects not only our emotional and mental well-being, but also our physical health as well. All aspects of our being suffer. When this happens, the way out becomes very difficult (though not impossible). The more years we ignore our voice of desire, the more it becomes necessary to clear our system of this poison, an issue we will discuss more in Chapter 6.

## The Art of Discernment

To discern which is the voice of desire and which are the voices born of tribal conditionings, you can think of the voice of desire as being the most juicy with life. And you can think of the competing voices as those belonging to ghosts. Yes, ghosts are alive, too. They are beings, also. However, ghosts are on the cusp: they are grey, flimsy, only partially manifested.

Living intentionally is being able to connect more and more with what is most alive in you.

You sense desire as the ocean—a vast, restorative body, teeming with life. The ghosts, while perhaps fascinating, no longer hold as much sway. The mystery of the ghosts has been solved; it's time to move forward. The ocean is where you want to go now, where you are pulled. You want to leave the ghosts behind. It's not that you hate the ghosts or curse the ghosts, but you no longer want to give them your attention and have them influence your action.

To live a life of intentional relationships—with yourself and with others—is to live a life where action is influenced, first and foremost, by desire. Again, this is contrary to the normative path, as well as contrary to what many spiritual and religious teachers will tell you. This is probably contrary to what your parents and elders have taught you. If you were raised in the Christian or Islamic religions, for instance, you were probably taught that desire is a trickster; you were probably taught that a desire for

God was good, but that all other desires are supposedly faulty, fruitless, and sinful. You were probably taught that you must sacrifice (repress) your own self, your own happiness, your own enjoyment, in order to attain the kingdom of God. Perhaps you followed this teaching for awhile... until one day you awakened, realizing that your own self was not divided from the kingdom of God but that *your self was the kingdom of God*! At this point, you made a radical break with the accepted dogma of your religion, and embarked on a new practice of self-inquiry. You went the way of the metaphysical rebels, the way of the mystics. You freed yourself. Continue to free yourself by honestly looking at your relationships! Are they as you desire?

Desire is a continuation on the journey of freedom. You know that acting on desire will require a sense of courage and a total trust in your own freedom, your own ability to take action and transform yourself. Further, you know that most people in this world do not have this, do not have the insight you have—and, because of this, you are called to be a leader. It is your job to show people the way. Show them that their praise of freedom as a virtue has been empty. Show them that true freedom is possible. Show them that desire is the call to adventure—and to adventure is to venture into the unknown, which takes courage. Share the truth Osho shared:

When you go into the uncharted sea, like Columbus did, there is fear, immense fear, because one never knows what is going to happen. You are leaving the shore of safety. You were perfectly okay, in a way; only one thing was missing— adventure. Going into the unknown gives you a thrill. The heart starts pulsating again; again you are alive, fully alive. Every fiber of your being is alive because you have accepted the challenge of the unknown.[26]

∞

## Practice: Lighting and Listening

In many Earth-based wisdom traditions, fire is crucial to spiritual evolution. Fire is seen as the element of desire, as well as that of death and rebirth. Fire transforms: It strips away all that is extraneous, providing new open spaces for regeneration. Fire is strong, hot—it is passion. Fire erupts and it spreads. After fire has cooled, we can see more clearly.

Just as many people have mistakenly learned to fear desire, so too have many come to fear fire. But fire is a friend. It is a tool for listening.

Light a fire. For this practice, the bigger and more wild the fire the better. If you can find an outdoor fire pit, that will be the most excellent choice. If you are unable to do this, an indoor fireplace or even just a candle will work, too.

Gaze into the fire. Allow the fire to cut through any clutter or confusion you may hold within you. Be totally in the moment, and focus only on your sensations: the feeling of the heat of the fire on your skin, the sound of the flames crackling and popping, the smell of the ashes in your nose. Watch the colors shift, from red to orange to blue to green…

As you gaze into the fire, be present and wait. Eventually, you will hear the voice of desire. (The amount of time this takes will vary from person to person. Be patient. Though it may take only a minute or two, allow yourself at least a few hours to experience this exercise. You don't want to feel rushed.)

This voice, though at first perhaps a bit startling, will calm your body. Your heart will have a sensation of warmth and there will be a balanced feeling throughout your entire bodily structure. In your mind, you will feel a sense of lightness and a sense of surety, a sense of deep wisdom. Continue to stare into the fire, and allow the emotion of gratitude to flow. Speak aloud now, vowing in the presence of the fire that you will take courage, and put into action what you have been told.

There is the chance, of course, that you may not hear the voice of desire on your first attempt at this practice. No worries. You may have to perform this several times before you tune into the voice of desire. Be patient with yourself. Discerning desire is an art that takes practice.

## In the Flow

A life well lived is a life that goes with the flow of desire. This is in contradiction with a life that suppresses desire.

To suppress desire is the normative way, the accepted way, the traditional way, the way of the majority of human beings on this planet. Sure, there are times when the tribe allows moments of desire—for example, the time of "falling in love" is an accepted part of the lifecycle in many parts of the world. However, those acceptable moments are always only allowed as brief moments. Even with falling in love, the people (it's usually assumed that there's only two, of the "opposite" sex) who fell in love must, eventually, snap out of it and "settle down" (for example: be monogamous, get married, purchase property, have children).

The tribe wants people to settle down because to be continually in love is dangerous: it is a threat to the normative functioning of the tribe. It is more difficult to send a person to war if they are in love; it is more difficult to lie to a person if they are in love; it is more difficult to persuade a person of some falsehood if they are in love—for being in love heightens a person's natural sensitivities.

For a person who loves, daily life is juicy; daily life is bursting with daring and mystery and truth—and so the opposite of that (fear) is easier to spot. This is why desire is not currently honored by the normative world. Desire leads to love—and not just romantic love, but love of self and love of whole planet and cosmos. In fact, desire holds the key to the current world's dissolution! And so it is no wonder that we are taught to repress desire.

When I fell in love with Rebecca, the whole world seemed to scream at me that I was flawed, that I was making a mistake, that I was being a disloyal partner to Andrew. At every turn, there were messages in the media and from the mouths of my well-meaning professors, friends, and family about how having only one lover was best. Because I hadn't yet discovered the concept of polyamory, because I hadn't yet discovered the dozens of books and countless websites on the possibility of loving many, I felt alone, confused, disoriented, and often disgusted with myself. I believed that love was scarce, and I worried that I was taking more than my fair share.

But when I sat down to meditate, either in the quiet park near the university or as I sat quietly in the bathtub at the end of the day, I repeatedly heard the unmistakable voice of desire. It was clear, it was loud, and to hide from it seemed a more frightening prospect than simply accepting it. The voice told me to be still and to trust, to know that the love I felt for Rebecca was not something to fear. My love for Rebecca was, rather, a doorway through which I must flow. The voice urged me to discard the conditioning of the media, the voices of my parents, teachers, and elders. The voice told me that the sexual desire I felt for Rebecca was a beautiful aspect of being drawn to her. The voice assured me that a communion with her would be beyond just orgasm or physical pleasure, but that we would become pure light itself. All I had to do now, the voice whispered, was be courageous. I had already been honest with Andrew about my love for her, but now I would need to be honest with others, too. I would need to come out of the closet. I would need to share my experience that it is possible to honestly and respectfully love more than one person simultaneously. My dawning love for Rebecca was the seed of the book you now hold in your hands. If I had repressed that voice of desire, you would not be reading this.

At the time, though, I felt like one of those Biblical prophets, whom upon hearing the command of God shrinks back, trembling: "Why *me*?" Instinctively, I knew the road ahead would not be easy. Even my love for Rebecca and Andrew would not keep me safe from attack, would not shield me from the anxieties of stepping beyond the bounds of normal. In short, I felt disoriented. I felt like I did not understand up from down, right from left. Everything was suddenly strange... I felt like I didn't know anything at all.

Being in the flow of love requires you to be courageous. There will be dark times ahead. In the next chapters, we will reflect on the very human craving for orientation, exploring how labels and categories are not as helpful as they appear to be.

# Chapter 3

# Beyond Orientation

*Life is full of uncertainties, full of surprises — that is its beauty! You can never come to a moment when you can say, "Now I am certain." When you say you are certain, you simply declare your death; you have committed suicide.*[27]

—*Osho*

## Categories and Normal Human Thinking

To use categories is a common way of thinking and communicating. If you say you are gay, straight, Puerto Rican, Vietnamese, male, female, Presbyterian, Buddhist, Hindu, wife, husband, mom, dad, or daughter, most people will recognize that common category. Through their recognition, they provide a sense of emotional and psychological security for you. The people to whom you tell your label will, with a knowing nod, affirm you as being *real*, as having a valid and recognizable existence, simply because that particular identity category is familiar, is known. Both the listener and the speaker perform this affirmation process (usually unconsciously).

Even if the listener's reaction to the speaker's category isn't positive (due to ignorance or prejudice), the speaker can then attempt to educate the listener about the nuances of that identity. Doing so can provide a slight boost to the speaker's ego — they perceive themselves in the teaching role and are therefore supposedly more knowledgeable than the listener. Egos and categories often support one another.

I have witnessed some of my well-meaning friends explain, in great detail, a long list of their relationship and sexual philosophies as well as intimate details about their various partnerships, in response to a blank stare when they say they are polyamorous (a label that is not yet widely known). No doubt a simple explanation such as "I have multiple partners" or "I believe love is abundant" might have sufficed, but, in normal human thinking, our minds have been conditioned to believe we must educate others. We must try to demonstrate that our chosen identity — whether it be our chosen religion, the gender we express through our clothing, or our favorite genre of music — is not just valid but that it is an advanced reality, a reality somehow above other realities.

Let me make it clear I have nothing against talking frankly about sexuality and relationships. I think it is vital that people openly share about their lives. What I am questioning is the tone and method in which these activists sometimes go about their dialogue — which is less of a dialogue and more of an attempt to invalidate the supposedly less-wise understanding of the other person. I believe it is impossible to start a true conversation, a conversation where all parties feel respected, that begins with the premise that one point of view is right and the other is wrong.

## Questioning Labels

In this chapter, I do *not* wish to claim that using categories and labels always bears negative results. Categories and labels can be quite practical, quite helpful. What I do intend is to critique the belief that a majority of human beings on this planet find to be true: that label-making is always empowering.

Labels are the root of much conflict. Labels disallow us in seeing our interconnected consciousness. Labels divide, and we forget we are One.

Indeed, the unintended outcome of placing too much importance on labels is that we do not connect as easily with others — which is a paradox, because we tend to think that labeling will help us connect better. Yet the opposite is often true. As Eckhart Tolle shares in *The Power of Now*, it is important for our spiritual practice to disidentify with the incessant mind, which is always coming up with labels and categories and concomitant worries, anxieties, fears, and prejudices. He explains how "identification with your mind creates an opaque screen of concepts, labels, words, judgments, and definitions that blocks all true relationship. It comes between you and yourself, between you and your fellow man and woman, between you and nature, between you and God. It is this screen of thought that creates the illusion of separateness, the illusion that there is you and a totally separate 'other.'"[28]

Through labels, we isolate our stories and experiences from other people's stories and experiences. And, although we don't intend to, the over-reliance upon labeling causes the consequence of dispossessing, in advance, a number of ecstatic, healing, and joyful experiences that we could have... all because we mistakenly believe we must "have" a fixed identity and fixed orientation.

The sexuality researcher Maria Pallotta-Chiarolli explores the interweavings of bisexuality and polyamory in *Border Sexualities, Border Families in Schools*. Citing prominent queer theorists such as Judith Butler and Jeffrey Weeks, she expresses mixed feelings about labels. On the one hand, she is grateful that labels can help unite people behind a common cause (such as the gay liberation movement, for example) and in constructing self-esteem and self-empowerment. On the other hand, she is concerned that labels can unintentionally encourage the construction of borders that welcome some inside but exclude and denigrate others.[29]

Labels can have the unintentional effect of creating new hierarchies, even among non-normative groups such as poly people. This problem can be seen in the common language I have heard used among some of my activist friends, when they say things like, "Oh, so-and-so is not a feminist, so she is not *really* polyamorous," or "That guy is only dating one person, so he is not *really* polyamorous." In statements like these, the speaker implicitly judges what a "real" poly person should look like, and excludes certain people from the club.

No doubt, labels such as gay, straight, and polyamorous are helpful for ordinary communication and for existing, in a mundane sense, in the daily world. If, for example, I moved to a new city and wanted to find friends, I would search online for poly meetups and queer-friendly spaces. Indeed, it would be much more difficult to locate potential new friends without utilizing the labels "poly" and "queer."

Further, it is indeed wonderful that we live in a time when, in a growing number of places across the globe, people can openly proclaim themselves gay or lesbian and the negative social consequences will be miniscule, or even nonexistent. We have indeed advanced as human beings. We have progressed far past the boundaries that many might have thought possible even twenty years ago. We are, on the whole, more compassionate, loving, and open to new ideas and new ways of being than ever before. This is indeed cause for celebration!

Simultaneously true, however, is the reality that there are significant drawbacks in using labels, identities, and categories as a primary mode of thinking and being in the world. To some, it might seem blasphemy to even ponder this idea, especially to those, for example, who have been toiling for years in the gay marriage movement and have worked very hard to gain what little ground they have. To critique the label gay, or any other label, for that matter, incites anger in many people.

Yet I believe that no institution and no paradigm and no idea should be above critique. To continually question appearances (even seemingly positive ones) is a key aspect to a spiritual path. What conclusion we make about the use of labels matters less than the simple willingness to peer closer, to question what might seem above reproach. As Osho writes, to be alive is to be continually open to surprise—or else we declare our own deaths.

## Identity and Orientation

What might be some of the drawbacks of categorical thinking? What are the consequences of thinking of oneself as "having" an identity?

In popular culture, the term identity is often linked to the term orientation. Sometimes the terms are even used synonymously. Identity and orientation are two words that are often merged in people's minds, and they are often used to explain either choices that are made or preferences that seem to be inborn. As the winds of sexual tolerance spread across the globe, many of us, more and more, are urged by therapists, popular authors, and even our friends and family to clearly define our identity. One of the main aspects in doing so is to "figure out" our sexual orientation and then proclaim that orientation to the world.

The concept of sexual orientation is very powerful. In the normal mainstream imagination, sexual orientation is seen as a positive force—because, supposedly, discovering and then acting upon one's innate sexual orientation is a key to a life of stability and happiness. Further, sexual orientation is often seen as the explanatory glue that holds all a person's sexual and relational choices together: Orientation is like the narrator in a film, calmly explaining the emotions and drives that fuel the characters' choices and actions. In sum, orientation is seen, as the term suggests, to orient. To direct.

Sexual orientation—often referred to as simply "orientation"—is commonly understood as a lifelong path. It is, supposedly, a journey we begin in adolescence, punctuated by key milestones, such as coming out of the closet, having one's first sexual encounter, or getting married. These moments are supposed to tell us who we are. We are gay, or we are not; we are a woman, or we are not; we are monogamous, or we are not; etc etc etc.

But what do these moments really mean? What can orientation really tell us about ourselves?

∞

## Practice: Reflecting on Love and Labels

Allow me to again quote Deborah Anapol's wise words:

> To me, the most important aspect of polyamory is not how many partners a person has. Rather, it is the surrendering of conditioned beliefs about the form a loving relationship should take and allowing love itself to determine the form most appropriate for all parties. If the truth is that two people freely embrace sexual exclusivity not because somebody made them do it or because they're afraid of the consequences of doing something else, I would still consider that couple polyamorous.[30]

Write a journal entry in response to this quotation. Write whatever you feel. After you have written all your emotions, reflect on and write answers to the following questions. Do you agree with Anapol's definition of polyamory? Why or why not? Have you allowed "love itself to determine the form" of your relationships? Why or why not?

## Your Path

The ultimate spiritual goal for every human is to discover, and then courageously live, their own path. This path is the path that will be full of challenges and spiritual lessons—all tailored to what each unique individual needs. It is what is needed for this lifetime. Not an easy path by any means, but a rewarding one—a path that reaps spiritual power, as well as feelings of wholeness, freedom and peace.

Yet how can that be? Is this not a paradox? If we are all One, if we are all an interconnected web of consciousness, then how can each person be totally unique and thus need to follow a totally unique path? Why would it be so important to choose one's own path, and not simply follow in the footsteps of others? Karen Armstrong, a mystic and scholar of world religions, is also puzzled by these questions. In her memoir *The Spiral Staircase,* she offers the concept of "the hero" —someone who lives a life based solely on intention.

> The great myths show that when you follow somebody else's path, you go astray. The hero has to set off by himself, leaving the old world and the old ways behind. He must venture into the darkness of the unknown, where there is no map and no clear route. He must fight his own monsters, not somebody else's, explore his own labyrinth, and endure his own ordeal before he can find what is missing in his life. Thus transfigured, he (or she) can bring something of value to the world that has been left behind. But if the knight finds himself riding along an already established track, he is simply following in somebody else's footsteps and will not have an adventure.[31]

The hero does not have it easy. The hero is continually tested, and is tempted to abandon the exploration in favor of what's easier: "an already established track." Therefore, the hero must be courageous. The hero must let go of all logic and be guided by intuition, the voice of desire. The hero must go forward without a map.

Heroes must face what is in front of them—which is, in the end, themselves. They each face their "own ordeal," something they themselves have actually *created*, because they know (at a subconscious level) exactly where they need to be and exactly what they need to experience in order to learn the lessons that need to be learned in this lifetime. Only by learning these very personally-specific lessons can the evolution of consciousness occur.

Every human has the potential to be a hero. Every. Single. One. I urge you to question the common wisdom that describes human beings as mostly selfish, deceitful, and violent creatures. We are not; you are not. Granted, there are times when some people do act selfishly, deceitfully, violently. This happens as a result of a perceived lack of power and options. People, especially those who live in poverty or who have been abused, act violently and deceptively because they feel they must do so in order to survive (whether physically or emotionally). As you are probably already aware, a tiny majority have continually controlled the world's resources... this imbalance is the root of the problems we see today, and it was the root of any problem you can read about in a history book.

The people who control the resources would have you believe that you, and your fellow human beings, are essentially flawed, essentially corrupt—therefore, certain laws and regulations have been put into place to "keep order." I urge you to question this worldview. I urge you to question the common belief that we need laws, police, and the military to keep people from going berserk. We do *not* need them.

At core, every human has the potential to be a hero, has the potential to lead a life of courage, of intention. Perhaps you are already on that path. What you need is simple, isn't it? You already know it, deep within your bones. *All you need is what you already have—to be yourself, to be free to act upon your voice of desire, and to be open to the unknown.*

When I feel fear at the prospect of change, I call to mind the Buddhist teaching of impermanence (*anicca*). This teaching explains that wealth, fame, status, health, beauty, and even relationships cannot bring a true sense of security. In truth, these things will come and these things will go. These things cannot really bring lasting security. *Everything* is impermanent; nothing lasts forever. The tree in your backyard, no matter how brilliant its leaves this summer, decades from now or even maybe hundreds of years from now, will eventually wither and pass into some new form. Mushrooms will grow, and the bark will decompose. Where there once was a tree now becomes a rose. Buddhism teaches that suffering is a result of clinging to any one form. We must realize each form is a temporary manifestation.

Everything changes. Everything moves. What seems certain today is nothing but a wisp of the wind tomorrow. Impermanence is a law of the universe that cannot simply be wished away. Therefore, identity labels such as gay, straight, monogamous, or polyamorous do not, in fact, have ultimate meaning. Impermanence teaches that *life is change,* and to pretend otherwise not only doesn't work—but it causes much suffering in the process.

If you wish to be a hero, if you wish to be a leader, if you wish to be a source of inspiration for others, then you will no longer place so much reverence upon labels and the concept of orientation. You will choose, instead, the forest of discovery, the ambiguous path without a map.

To face into the darkness of uncertainty, and move forward nonetheless.

To face into the darkness of impermanence, and have courage nonetheless.

To face into the darkness of ambiguity, and make choices nonetheless.

∞

## Practice: Reflecting on False Promises

In normative culture, people are offered a whole host of false promises. These promises assure that the law of impermanence is not a law at all. These promises come in the form of cultural institutions, contracts, popular books and media, advertisements, or clichés. Some of the more obvious examples of these include weddings, weather predictions, or the buying and selling of insurance.

Dedicate a week to observation. As you go about your life, note in your journal every single event, moment, situation, or social tradition you encounter that subtly or not-so-subtly promises that you can have a stable, predictable, unchanging life. At the end of the week, review the list. Reflect on the very common human urge to try to make certain what cannot be certain. Do your best not to judge those who propagated those promises, but rather, note in yourself how you—whether currently or in the past—have craved these kinds of assurances. Reflect on why it is so tempting to want to declare, as Osho writes, "Now I am certain."

Sit for a few minutes in silence. As you breathe in, silently say the words "not knowing." As you breathe out, say "beautiful."

## A New Orientation

The concept of sexual orientation, as queer researcher Sara Ahmed notes, is misleading, because it is built upon the faulty premise that each of us are born—and therefore destined—to feel certain ways. She believes, and I agree, that the concept of sexual orientation is, ultimately, a fantasy.

> Indeed, orientation is a powerful technology insofar as it constructs desire as a magnetic field: it can imply that we were drawn to certain objects and others *as if* by a force of nature: so women are women insofar as they are oriented toward men... The fantasy of natural orientation is an orientation device that organizes worlds around the form of the hetero-sexual couple, as if it were from this "point" that the world unfolds...[32]

In contrast to this normal way of viewing orientation, Ahmed creates a new definition. Orientation should not just denote sexual object choice—rather, orientation should be seen more broadly. Orientation should be seen "as involving differences in one's very relation to the world—that is, in how one 'faces' the world or is directed toward it."[33]

With this new definition, many possibilities open. We can see orientation not as being what gender we are typically attracted to, but rather we can see orientation as our general approach to life. And, the term gains spiritual power for us as we begin to use it as a ground for making choices.

Instead of thinking of orientation narrowly as who we are attracted to or who we want to have sex with, what about thinking of orientation as the backbone for living an intentional life, a life that departs from the normal way of greed, competition, and scarcity? What if we thought of orientation as helping us reflect upon whether the action we are about to make is an action of love and compassion? If we viewed orientation as our "very relation to the world," how might our relationships change? How might we approach our love lives? Our family? Our friendships? Instead of orientation as a fixed inborn tendency, what about orientation as the amalgamation of the choices we make on a daily basis, which creates a certain flow for our lives? What if orientation was no longer something supposedly handed down to us by our biology, but instead, what if orientation was something *entirely within our control*?

If orientation was not something that happened to us, but rather orientation as something we daily choose... how, then, would we orient ourselves? How, then, would we act?

## Beyond Forms

To take these insights a step further—to truly intend to go beyond the normative paradigm of orientation—one then ventures into a territory that is, perhaps, even more challenging. If we can release our over-reliance upon labels and also get beyond the normal way of thinking about orientation, we come to the insight that attachment to *all forms* is a hindrance to spiritual growth.

Why do we reject some as relationship partners, yet accept others? Why are we drawn to some and repulsed by others? Why are we initially pulled toward some that we wouldn't expect, but then later run away? What is the voice that tells us that a particular person is attractive, intriguing, sexy, ugly, unappealing, or our type? Could it be that that voice is actually the voice of the tribe, the voice of cultural conditioning?

In *A Course in Love: Powerful Teachings on Love, Sex, and Personal Fulfillment*, Joan Gattuso cautions us that we have received many messages from our culture about physical appearance that do not always correspond to the messages in our own hearts, and do not always lead us to the people who will be most beneficial for our lives. If we are truly intent upon the evolution of our consciousness, we can no longer be bound by superficiality; we must begin to perceive at a deeper level. Physical build, clothes, hairstyle—these do not matter. Gattuso teaches that we must be courageous enough to perceive inner beauty, to be able to enter into a relationship with someone based not upon how they look, but to base one's criteria on the quality and compatibility of spirit.

There is another way to perceive yourself and all others. It begins by experiencing an instant of seeing beyond the body. Then later you glimpse it more frequently, seeing the lovely, seeing through the outer envelope into the inner splendor. You come to know that in the end only this larger sphere is real. Everything else has been but shadowy figures inhabiting our disconnected dreams.

Once we release ourselves from the misperception that we are only bodies, we no longer wish to imprison others in the place from which we have escaped. The obsession with the body is gladly released in favor of the radiance of the inner spirit. The love of God calls us to recognize the spirit in one another and to no longer identify our brothers and sisters as solely their bodies. The attraction of the spirit is irresistible once we have become comfortable enough to let our guard down and explore our depths... The world we see is built on whether we see the physical or the spiritual as the real world. When we choose the physical, we can never escape seeing the body as our reality. When we choose the spiritual, all of heaven bows down to bless us. Then we will see the physical world truly through the eyes of Spirit.[34]

Gattuso discusses the opportunities for love, romance, and connection that are lost when people make judgments based upon the inconsequential aspects of physical appearance and age. I would add to her insights that judging based upon other factors, such as gender, ethnicity, and level of income (or any other material form), will inadvertently cause one to overlook many potentially wonderful partners, friends, and intimates.

Being open to people is a rare practice in the world of the normal, but it is a vital practice in service of an orientation that has compassion and love, as well as a sense of adventure and curiosity at its core.

∞

## Practice: Speaking with Signlessness

When I met Robert, I didn't truly see him.

We both attended a party hosted by a mutual friend. Robert approached me, introduced himself, and told me I was beautiful. Apparently, I said thank you, giggled, and walked away. I don't remember this. All I have is a vague memory of glancing at what seemed to be an odd-looking hybrid of a hippie and a biker: long flowing hair, leather, and lots of tattoos. Quite simply, Robert didn't register as a potential mate, or even a potential friend for that matter. His form wasn't appealing to me.

Months later, we met again, at the home of another mutual friend. And then we met again, and again. We never planned these meetings. One evening, I noticed him, building a fire. I came and stood nearby, helping feed logs into the massive blaze. We didn't say a word except hello, but I had the strange feeling that we were becoming friends. I liked his energy. Then, many months later, we were sitting next to each other at a meditation workshop. He got up for a few minutes to use the restroom. While he was gone, I put my legs up on his chair. When he returned, he asked politely (and somewhat timidly) if I wanted to rest my legs on him. So I did. A few minutes later, when he placed his hands on my feet, I felt an electric current rise up from the base of my spine and shoot out the crown of my head. I felt the love begin. The next time we met, I no longer noticed the leather or tattoos... I began to see the Robert that had been there, the whole time, all those months. I had failed to see him for so long— but then, suddenly, I did. His touch woke me up, out of my superficial, judgmental slumber.

In Buddhism, the teaching/practice of looking beyond the material form is called *animitta*, which means signlessness. When we practice *animitta*, we look beyond the sign. We look beyond the outer form, and perceive at a deeper level.

Here is an exercise for looking deeper. Find an acquaintance— someone you don't know very well. Choose someone you have dismissed as a potential friend or lover because some aspect of their physical form or some aspect of identity appears to clash with what you typically like. Maybe you judged this person to have terrible taste in clothing. Or maybe you noticed this person has brown or missing teeth. Or maybe this person's age is far younger or far older than yours. Maybe this person has an accent that you find difficult to understand, or maybe this person's skin color is not the same as yours.

Set up a time to meet with this person. Share tea together, or even a meal.

Talk to this person. *Really talk. Really listen.* Drop all masks and ignore the clock. Melt into the moment. Allow yourself to *just be* in this person's presence. Listen to this person's words not just with your logical mind, but, focusing on your breath as you listen, *feel* this person's words as well as this person's being-ness. Feel their moods, as they relate a story. Feel their personality, as they describe their lives. Drop all labels and judgments. Ask yourself, silently: *Who* is this person? What can I learn? What beauty is here?

## The Adventurous Life

As you open your heart, acting with courage and compassion as your central motivations, you will find that your relationships change. You will no longer cling to labels, to categories. You will begin to encounter people in a totally new way.

As these shifts happen, you may find that your life begins to lose some of its typical borders. You may suddenly find yourself spending time with different kinds of people, perhaps even people you previously would have been embarrassed to be seen with. At first, you might be terrified, wondering what others think. You may be at the grocery store with your new lover or at the library with your new friend, and bump into someone from work, or perhaps a neighbor you respect… and your heart may momentarily skip a beat or your hands may begin to shake. Be patient with yourself! Be prepared that it may take some time to feel accustomed to seeing beyond the physical form; and, it may take some time to de-program yourself from anxiously wondering what others think of you.

As this de-programming happens, you will find yourself with choices to make. Love may be abundant, but time is not. With whom will you spend your time? From whom will you learn? Who will be the recipients of your energy? What people will inspire you to act courageously? And, how will you treat these people? How might you practice courage and compassion in your everyday life?

# Chapter 4

# Beyond Jealousy

*How am I to live*
*In such prosperity?*

*Sharing everything*
*Still*
*My cup*
*Overflows*
*& I receive more*
*It appears to me*
*Than I ever give.*
—Alice Walker[35]

## A Dream of Fear

The night before I began to write this chapter, I had a dream. In the dream, I was making love with a beautiful man. This man told me he had a polyamorous agreement with his wife; he told me his wife knew about me and was happy. I believed what this man told me.

While we were enjoying sex, his wife came into the bedroom followed by a jeering crowd. She began to shout at me, calling me "whore." The crowd hissed and booed. Her husband tried to defend me, but she silenced him. After shouting at me for quite some time, she fell silent for a moment, panting for breath. I finally found my voice. I began to talk gently about love. As I began to speak about forgiveness, a few men in the crowd, towering men with bulging muscles, began to rush towards me. Their faces were flushed with disgust, and they were pounding their fists into their hands and growling. They shouted: "You must pay for what you've done!" The crowd cheered in agreement. Realizing that my words of love were falling on deaf ears, I began to run. I ran past the outstretched arms of the crowd, out the back door of the house. As I passed a stranger on the street, I tried to scream for help, but my words were barely a whisper.

I awoke from the dream, heart pounding. I only had to reflect a few moments, because the meaning of the dream was obvious: There was, and is, still fear in my heart. I fear for human beings. I still sometimes doubt whether humanity is ready to be reborn to a new paradigm of love.

The muscled men in the dream represent all those people throughout history who have been openly hostile, and even violent, to ways of loving that defy what is normal. And, dear reader, I admit: On my worst days, I look to the sky in a state of confusion and despair. *Why*, I ask, do so many people still despise gays and lesbians? *Why*, I ask, do people feel such shame when their bodies are pulled to more than one lover? *Why*, I ask, are people so afraid of their own hearts?

As I climbed out of bed that morning, I said a prayer of thanks to the universe for sending me the dream. In my journey thus far as a poly author and speaker, I sometimes, unfortunately, have been impatient with those who are interested in hearing the lessons I have to teach but who are yet unwilling (for a multitude of reasons) to enact those lessons in their daily lives. My empathy is not there, sometimes. The dream reminded me of my own lingering fears and insecurities. Through the dream, I was able to renew my intention for empathy, I was able to remember just how difficult it is to face—and then transform—the inadequacy, confusion, frustration, sadness, and jealousy that stem from the normative paradigm of viewing people/relationships as possessions.

In the dream, the husband saw the wife as an object he could manipulate—by keeping his relationship with me a secret, he was, in effect, releasing himself of the terror of having a potentially hard conversation with her. By avoiding that conversation, he was running from the possibility that, upon hearing about his love for me, she might become upset and perhaps even want to leave the relationship. By not telling her the truth of his heart, he was denying her humanity, thus reducing her to an object, to a thing. He gave her no choice, no input on the matter. His lie forced her (for awhile) to believe the false truth that he wished to be sexually and romantically intimate with only her.

The wife in the dream saw her husband as a possession, too. She believed he belonged to her and only her. Accordingly, she did not direct her anger toward the possession: for, in her mind, her husband was not actually a full human being, but rather an object without the power to make choices. This was why her anger was directed at me, the perceived thief. I had taken her object; it was my fault.

## The Garden

To begin to view our partners, lovers, and even our friends and family as free beings can be difficult. If we saw them as free, perhaps they might fall in love with someone else, or perhaps they might leave. The fear of abandonment is strong within most human beings.

The metaphor of a garden helps us understand how to practice freedom and non-possession. If we tend to a garden, we may purchase the seeds, plant the seeds, and tend to the plants. We water; we weed; we harvest. But even though we direct so much loving intention toward the garden, we do not truly control the garden, and we do not truly control the Earth. We may love them, yes; we may look after them—yet, in the end, it is up to the seeds whether they will manifest into leaves, it is up to the sun whether it will shine, it is up to the animals whether they will eat the plants or leave them alone. Though we may love the garden and the whole Earth upon which the garden depends, all of these are out of our control. We do not possess the garden;

we do not truly own it. The most we can do is feel grateful for the time we have to care for and enjoy the garden. Each morning we can wake up, look at the garden, and smile. Even when the time comes for change, we can feel grateful. For example, if we choose to move to another city, we may have to leave the garden behind. However, that does not mean we no longer love it. We can still feel love and gratitude for the garden, knowing that, despite the physical distance, the garden has touched our lives. We will always love the garden.

In the same way we remember that the garden is not our possession, we can also remember that people are not our possession. We can feel grateful that we have been able to care for them, yet we can also understand that they are free. They have always been free.

## Waking Up to Freedom

The mental illusion that a person "belongs" to us is simply that: an illusion. In truth, we have no power over another person. Sure, we can nag, persuade, or even manipulate a person to do something we want them to do. But, at core, all people are free. They have always been free and they will always be free. We cannot truly control another person. Even if a person agrees to do something after we attempt to persuade them, we have not *caused* that person to do something. Yes, our persuasive efforts may have been an aspect in that person's thought processes—yet, the person was the one who put the choice into action. We did not "make" that person do anything. That person chose to do what they did. That is the responsibility of free will.

Therefore, just as we cannot control another, no one can control you. You are free. Moreover, no one can "give" you freedom. Freedom is already yours, forever.

Granted, there is ethical behavior and there is unethical behavior. We must discuss that facet when we engage in the question of free will. Let us return to my dream example. The husband misused his freedom to act unethically: he lied to both his wife and myself. The husband was practicing non-consensual non-monogamy (probably the most common form of non-monogamy on our planet at this time), because he was using lies to pursue another lover without giving his wife any say in the matter.

By contrast, ethical non-monogamy would involve the husband being honest with his wife from the beginning. The husband, upon feeling the first twinges of desire, could have sat down with his wife, held her hand, and spoke from his heart.

Nonetheless, it is important to remember that the husband, by the simple fact that he was a human being, had the freedom to make a choice. As a human being, he had the power to choose his own path. His wife, after finding out the lie, had a choice, too. It was up to her whether or not to forgive her husband. Further, she had the choice whether or not to request changes in the relationship or to leave it altogether. We all have choices—that is our power as human beings. No one can control us. Even if we believe we are "allowing" someone to control us (the government, our employer, our family, etc.), we are actually just fooling ourselves. No one controls another person.

At the core of each human being is an immense indwelling of power. A human may be asleep to that power—nonetheless, it is still there.

## Jealousy and Being

When enlightened teachers say they have gone beyond jealousy, what is it that they mean? Do they really mean that they *never* feel jealous? Does it mean they are repressed or defective, somehow blocking or lacking very basic human emotions?

Hearing that someone is no longer stressed by the feeling of jealousy often creates in the mind of the hearer a combination of disbelief, as well as a flicker of hope. As jealousy is a painful emotional state, the idea that one can be rid of it—or at least partially rid of it—is an incredibly uplifting, but also strangely disorienting thought. Jealousy seems hard-wired, natural. How can a human being go beyond jealousy? Is it possible? To answer these questions and to begin to understand the phenomenon of going beyond jealousy, one must first realize what jealousy truly is.

When analyzing emotions, it is good to first make the distinction between jealousy and envy. These words are not the same. Jealousy is the fear and terror of loss; envy is a desire to possess what someone else possesses (or seems to possess). However, jealousy and envy both have the same root cause. Jealousy and envy are a result of temporarily forgetting the interconnectedness of all beings. When we feel jealous or envious, we mistakenly believe that the joyful thing is happening for that "other person" or those "other people," but it's not happening for us. We feel we cannot tap into the joy. We feel separate. We feel lacking. We feel empty, or even worthless. We perceive that we are not participating in the joy, in the awesomeness of what is going on; we feel that we are not included.

A jealous feeling is, at root, a manifestation of fear. When the wife in the dream called me a whore, she was reacting out of fear. She was afraid she was going to lose her husband. She felt fear that her husband loved me more than he loved her. She was so full of fear.

*Compersion* is a term that was coined by the polyamory movement in the 1990s. Compersion means the opposite of jealousy. Compersion is feeling joy because someone else is feeling joy, regardless of the particular *source* of that person's joy. (In other words, that person's joy might seem to have nothing at all to do with you.) By actively cultivating compersion, we are able to release ourselves from feeling like jealousy and envy is our nature state: We can evolve our consciousness.

Practicing compersion is not always easy, and it can be a long process to overcome jealousy. You may not even be able to fully overcome jealousy in this lifetime. That's okay. Be patient with yourself. To begin to practice compersion does not mean that you will automatically become immune to jealousy; it is, rather, that you will learn how to skillfully deal with jealousy if/when it manifests.

Here is an illustration of compersion. Susan, a professor at a university, gets her article published in a prestigious journal. Susan is so happy! So, of course, she tells her dear friend and colleague, Jonathan. When Jonathan hears the news, he recalls that he himself has been trying to get published in that same journal—but to no avail. Jonathan now has a choice. He can become overwhelmed by jealous feelings, or he can choose to cultivate happy feelings for his dear colleague. To choose the former choice is to erect a barrier between himself and Susan, a situation of suffering. To choose the latter choice is to choose compersion, a practice that draws both friends together in a sense of camaraderie, a sense of collaboration, a sense of excitement about the possibilities of life. Thus, compersion is a sharing. All parties benefit emotionally and spiritually.

Many people find the concept of compersion incredibly difficult to swallow, though. This is especially the case when they think about it within the context of their romantic and sexual relationships. It's one thing, people say, to be compersive about a colleague's success, but it's quite another to feel happy about your partner being intimate with someone other than you. Yet, it is possible to cultivate compersion in any social situation, even the most difficult. The book *Spiritual Polyamory* explains how compersion in a romantisexual context can be understood through the analogy of friendship.

If… you think in terms of having multiple friendships, you may be able to better understand the philosophy of a spiritual approach to polyamory. For example, you can most likely appreciate that if you have a friend who makes a new friend, that doesn't have to pose a threat to the relationship you have with your friend. You want that person to be happy. You can therefore practice compersion, the opposite of jealousy, which states that you gain happiness when those you care about are happier. This involves non-attachment to your ego's goals of having everyone to yourself. Once you are able to see how sexual possession has became an "accepted attachment" in your society, you can then introduce sexuality into the above "multiple friendship" scenario, and see how your responsibility to yourself is to release your attachments as opposed to struggling to preserve them.[36]

To be in touch with one's true nature is to be in touch with the simple yet mind-blowing fact that you, we, each of us, are not separate from anyone. There is no "other." We are all interrelated—and not just in a metaphoric sense, but actually and really.

If your lover makes love with someone else… it is not actually that this person is a someone else. Rather, your lover makes love to that person—*and also with the whole entire universe!* You are included in that universe. There is no true separation, though it may often seem so to our limited human minds. This is one of the core Tantric teachings in the ancient Sanskrit texts.[37] That love and sexual connection may sometimes *seem* as though it is taking place between only the bodies present in the bed—but, in reality, that love and connection can be felt throughout and by the whole cosmos. It is just that we need to learn to perceive this, it is just that we need to open our minds to the reality of how the universe works.

To realize the inherent unity of all beings is to singlehandedly negate the power and the pull of jealousy. The emotion becomes obsolete. Such a shift in perspective takes a tremendous amount of courage—at first. But, over time, it becomes easy to see that compersion (not jealousy) is the true nature of loving.

∞

## Practice: Feeling Compersion

Compersion takes practice. Just as lying is (implicitly or explicitly) taught in our societies, so too is jealousy. Jealousy is seen as an acceptable or even a healthy response, especially in the context of romantic relationships. If jealousy is not felt, sometimes a partner may even assume that real love is not present within the relationship.

Because the dust of jealousy has been so deeply ingrained, compersion is a practice that must be cultivated. Learning it will be a process. Be patient with yourself; tiny steps are wonderful.

Visit a public place. This could be a community pool, park, festival, or restaurant. Go to where people are gathered, having fun and simply enjoying being alive. Watch for those people who are reveling in their relationships. Keep your eyes open for the mother holding the hands of her two sons, as they skip and play. Keep your ears open for the laughter of the couple, who snuggle together on the bench, whispering secrets only they know. Find the people who seem the most alive with each other. Look, listen, and sense, while being as unobtrusive as possible. (In other words, avoid blatant staring. Your goal is to perceive and observe, not create an environment for others that feels uncomfortable or unsafe.) Reflect on how the loving, intimate scenes before you are not seeming to include you—yet, at the same time, *you are included.*

Open to the love around you. Let it absorb into your being, and simultaneously reflect your own love and gratitude outward, toward everyone present. Silently thank those you watch, for they are your teachers today.

Consciously focus on your breath. With every inhale, silently say, "compersion, breathing in." With every exhale, "abundance, breathing out." Or, use your own words: with every inhale and exhale use a phrase that reminds you of the interconnectedness of all beings and the abundance of love available to all.

## Compersion and Unconditional Love

When compersion is manifested, there is a related energy that assists and accompanies compersion. This energy is unconditional love.

Unconditional love helps compersion to manifest. It is difficult to say whether unconditional love first creates the feeling of compersion, or whether compersion begins the feeling of unconditional love. While this question is interesting to the logical mind, the answer matters less than simply putting into practice these two types of being.

Caroline Myss refers to unconditional love as "conscious love," a kind of love "which makes the heart a universal instrument of goodness without private agendas that can reduce love to acts of manipulation and attempts to control others."[38] Because we live in a world that values lying rather than honesty and control rather than freedom, living by a code of unconditional love can seem incredibly challenging. It goes against the "common sense" of the normal. To adopt unconditional love as a value in your life is a choice that takes intention, that takes courage. The road ahead will not be easy, and probably very few people will understand, let alone support, your choice. To love your lovers, partners, friends, family, and neighbors unconditionally, without assumptions or expectations or conditions or limits, is so far from the norm that if you begin to act this way, many will believe you are crazy, and will spend a good amount of time trying to warn you about the naïvety of your actions and beliefs. You will be told that to love unconditionally will cause you pain.

In the poem "The Manoeuvre," William Carlos Williams evokes that sense of risk, that sense of courage in doing the non-normal thing, the non-expected thing.

I saw two starlings
coming in toward the wires.
But at the last,
just before alighting, they

turned in the air together
and landed backwards!
that's what got me—to
face into the wind's teeth.[39]

The starlings could have landed in the typical way. But the birds chose what was more difficult. The poet did not predict this. The poet, watching the scene, and feeling perhaps calm contentment, suddenly feels his heart leap! *Look at what is possible,* the poet thinks. *Look at all the wonderful things I don't understand and could never predict.* Even though the poet had expectations about how the birds would land, he was open to feeling the joy about *not* having his expectations fulfilled. That is being awake, being open.

The poet's joyous reaction is a good example of both compersion and unconditional love. The poet loved the birds unconditionally, regardless of the choices they could make. The poet practiced compersion because he was happy with the choice that the starlings made. And, the starlings, just being who they were and doing what they did, changed the poet. The poet drew inspiration from the birds' uncanny flight; it affected him. An intentional action, a courageous action, an action that defies expectations and norms, ripples outward. Others feel the ripples, and they begin asking questions about their own lives and about what is possible.

Making the commitment to unconditional love is an intentional action. It will take courage; it will take daring. It will be one of the most challenging, yet utterly rewarding practices you can undertake. To be unconditional in your love is to be like the starlings, flipping backwards… doing something different.

To practice compersion is to practice unconditional love; to practice unconditional love is to practice compersion. The two states are so deeply linked that, in some ways, they can be considered synonymous. By enacting one, you enact the other.

## Unconditional Love: Desire and Crisis

Unconditional love is what people want. It is what people are searching for, whether they know it or not. To have a person or multiple people who love us, no matter what: no matter our flaws, our mistakes, our foibles and our fuck-ups—wonderful! It's what we want. Deep down, in the core of every human being, there is a desire for unconditional love.

Many people claim they live by the principle of unconditional love. Terms like unconditional love tend to get tossed around as lip service, yet many people do not actually practice them or truly understand *how* to love unconditionally. There are also many people who laugh in cynical mockery at the supposed naïvety of the polyamorous who practice compersion. These people who laugh often give the following logical argument: To desire (whether emotionally or physically) another person outside of a committed partnership creates a "diluted" relationship, a flawed and bad relationship where everyone just gets a small piece of the puzzle of love and no one is fully happy. Dossie Easton and Janet W. Hardy, authors of *The Ethical Slut: A Practical Guide to Polyamory, Open Relationships & Other Adventures* (the most referenced book on polyamory) call this kind of thinking "starvation economies," which contrast with abundance economies. In starvation economies, people believe they must fight and compete for love, sex, intimacy, and relationships because there isn't enough to go around. In such a fear-based way of thinking, compersion seems not only ridiculous but impossible.[40]

I can attest, however, that there are many people, among them my close friends, family, and colleagues, who could not imagine living any other way than the way of abundant love. To love openly does *not* create diluted love—on the contrary, to love openly, with an expectation of abundance, is to exponentially raise the energy of love for all involved. For many spiritual teachers and polyamorous people worldwide, compersion is not just a lofty ideal, but it is a daily practice.

Practicing compersion is to bring light to the idea that jealousy is *not* love energy, but it is actually fear energy. Osho offers an antidote to this fear energy: love. He writes: "If you feel there is fear in your being, love more. Be courageous in love, take courage. Be adventurous in love; love more, and love unconditionally, because the more you love the less will be the fear."[41]

Many people pay lip service to unconditional love, yet they often simultaneously maintain the conditions that their lover must love only them, must desire only them. Over time, as the relationship settles, these conditions can be difficult to adhere to, especially as the new relationship energy begins to soften. (New relationship energy, or NRE for short, is a term from the poly movement. NRE is that sexy-awesome-sparkly-feeling at the beginning of a relationship; it's that initial whirlwind of rainbows and sunshine when first falling in love.)

If partners place these kinds of conditions, then guilt can often arise if one or both partners feels an attraction outside the relationship. This situation is incredibly difficult. On the one hand, there have been vows, there have been promises. Or maybe the agreements have been tacit, unspoken, merely assumed. No matter the individual specifics, however, if unconditional love is not present, then there will be suffering.

∞

## Practice: Being Honest About Love

Reflect on the course of your life thus far. Have you ever felt desire for multiple people at the same time? (Think of the term *desire* in a broad way—this could be desire on a sexual/physical level, or it could mean desire on spiritual, emotional, or intellectual levels.) Compose a journal entry about this desire. Answer the question: Did this desire either support or clash with the principles of unconditional love and abundance? Were you honest with the important people in your life about this desire, or did you keep it a secret? Why? What was the outcome of your honesty or your lack of honesty? How did the desire you felt then affect you now?

## Compersion and Compassion in Uncertain Times

Compersion is another way of saying empathy. We have discussed cultivating empathy when a loved one or partner feels a desire to connect with someone else. Another challenging opportunity to practice compersion is when there is an argument, disagreement, or confusion between yourself and your loved one.

There may be a time when you are asked to leave your loved one alone. This can be very difficult to agree to, because intense emotions are circulating. In this situation, your loved one may become very confused, sad, angry, or some other difficult emotion, and request to take space away from you. This space may range from a few minutes to a few hours, or maybe even a few weeks or months. Often, your loved one will not even know how long it will take before what is blooming inside them is ready to be harvested. They will come to you, often with downcast eyes and a heavy heart, saying, "I need some time and space." Your loved one may even go so far as to say that they are unsure as to the future of the relationship. They may even say, "I don't know if we should continue our relationship."

What often makes this situation incredibly difficult is that you may want nothing more than to talk—*at the exact moment the request for space is being made.* And, you may be jealous (insecure) of the time and space your loved one needs—because you want your loved one to need *you* rather than the time and space! You may feel an urgency to settle the matter, to hash it all out, even though you rationally understand that now is not the best time for such a discussion because it does take at least two consenting people in a calm state of mind to have a productive conversation.

What they are asking for is, essentially, compassion. They are asking you to patiently give space in order that they may travel deep inside, and explore in a way that does not allow for a companion. *It is vital to the health of the relationship that you agree to your loved one's request.* In order to understand how this is so, imagine for a moment the reverse situation. Imagine that you needed space and time apart from your loved one—but they denied your request. What feelings would arise in you? Would you feel imprisoned? Frustrated? Annoyed? Angry? Misunderstood? Unloved? Objectified? Since you yourself would like the freedom to take space and time if you needed it, then it is reasonable that granting the same sense of freedom to your loved one is crucial. (Of course, it needs to be mentioned that if the initial request for space/time is made in anger or by using violent language, you have every right to state how you feel, and then request that the request be framed differently, explaining to your loved one that you would feel more at peace with granting the request if the words carrying that request were spoken with kindness.)

Another reason that such a request can be incredibly difficult to deal with is that this kind of request often triggers feelings of pain and betrayal, especially if there has been a public commitment ritual (a wedding or handfasting, for example) where you both agreed to be each other's constant companion throughout life. So, if your partner asks for space away from you, it may seem like a violation of the loving promises made. Images may come flooding forth into your mind—images of happy times or declarations made in the heat of romance. Your emotions may feel like they are sinking and swirling into a sort of doomed flurry; you may be interpreting this request symbolically, seeing this request for space as representing the loss of your dearest companion.

If it is your aim to live a life of intention, it will be necessary to peacefully acquiesce to such a request. Even though you may be filled with doubt, anxiety, or even terror at the prospect of losing your loved one, it will be necessary for you to say Yes. It will be necessary to open your arms and let your dear one walk away.

∞

## Practice: Feeling What You Are Feeling

While waiting for your loved one to return or contact you, it will be vital to *fully feel* all the emotions that are arising within you. This is true whether your loved one needs to take a ten-minute walk alone or whether your loved one has moved thousands of miles away. The challenge is not to run from the emotions, not to repress them. If you fail to engage with your emotions, you will not have a clear energetic system when your loved one is ready to talk.

Many people in this situation might be tempted to simply get their mind off the situation by distracting themselves with work, hobbies, or even destructive behaviors such as eating junk food or drinking alcohol. If you aim to live a life of intention, it is crucial that you do not lower your energies by succumbing to the temptation to numb yourself.

The goal will actually be to do what feels most frightening — run face forward *into* your emotions. Be prepared: Once you make the conscious choice not to run, you may then be flooded with even more intense feelings. At this point, you may be tempted to retreat into the numbing strategies I mentioned above. Yet I urge you to continue moving forward into the fire. Treat this moment in your life as an experiment, trusting that you cannot and will not die from feeling emotions; rather, the emotions are there to allow you to enter a new state of consciousness. *The emotions are useful for your evolution.*

Once you can fully experience the emotions without resistance and without judgment, you will be able to touch a state of calm awareness, where it will be much easier to patiently wait for your loved one to contact you. As you practice the following walking meditation, you will be able to feel a certain wholeness while simultaneously embracing the terror of your feelings—a paradox indeed! As the renowned Quaker teacher Parker J. Palmer has written, "Wholeness does not mean perfection: it means embracing brokenness as an integral part of life."[42]

Take a gentle walk. Outdoors is best for this, but if the weather is inhospitable, you can simply clear a path inside your home.

Walk slowly and deliberately, as if you were trying to walk across a body of water that you were not sure had completely frozen over; you don't want to step too roughly, lest the ice should break. Each step is careful. Each step is meaningful.

For the first few minutes, simply focus on your breathing. Feel your breath sync up with the movement of your arms and legs in whatever way feels natural to you. Then, say silently to yourself: "I allow whatever emotions need to arise in me." Continue to walk. As emotions come slowly one by one—or perhaps flood your system very quickly—keep walking, carefully and deliberately, moving your arms and legs in a rhythmic, steady pattern. Use the forward movement as a symbolic embodiment of the fact that you are not afraid of your emotions, but rather *you step into them.*

If at any time the emotions become too intense, silently say to yourself: "All human beings have emotion." Repeat this as many times as you need to. In this way, you remove yourself from the drama of the situation and become an observer of the emotions rather than feeling gripped by them. By reminding yourself that all human beings experience emotion, whether positive or negative, you remember that it is useless to wish that emotions did not happen. You also recall what you have in common with other human beings, thus creating a sense of empathy and compassion rather than isolation. You are not alone. We all feel and deal with emotions. Yes, what you are going through may be difficult, but you are evolving your consciousness by embracing your emotions in a meditative, reflective way, rather than running from them.

By practicing this walking meditation, you will be more likely to greet your loved one, when they return, with peace and stillness in your heart. You will be ready for an open and honest conversation.

## Moving Forward

To begin to view emotions like jealousy as a tool for transformation is not the ordinary, normal way. It takes guts. Jealousy and other challenging emotions will test your heart, test your resolve.

At this time on the planet, you are in the minority. Although you may feel increasing freedom and increasing creativity and zest for life, you may also feel at times that the number of people who truly understand what you are doing is shrinking. You may feel lonely. In the next chapter, we will move forward, together, courageously finding and cultivating relationships where the underlying principle is abundance.

# Chapter 5

# New Energy Investments

*When a log that has only just started to burn is placed next to one that is burning fiercely, and after awhile they are separated again, the first log will be burning with much greater intensity.*
—Eckhart Tolle[43]

## Finding Wholeness

Once your intention is to move headlong into your fears, move headlong into exploring the uncertain territories of orientation and jealousy, you may soon realize the necessity of connecting with like-minded people. As you make your way on this non-normal path, it may be very difficult, if not impossible, for you to put your newfound philosophies into practice without the help of loving companions. People who are brave like you.

To recognize the essential oneness inherent in the very structure of the universe is to recognize that our solitary spiritual practice—whether it be meditation, journaling, gardening, hiking, surfing, yoga, Reiki, or whatever it may be—is meaningless if we do not carry the insights we learned and the peace of mind we obtained while alone out into the greater world. Through commingling with loving others that we *intentionally choose*, we will alternate between teaching and being taught. We will alternate between sharing our visions and receiving the visions of others. Only through the social integration of the wisdom gained through solitude will we finally feel whole.

Parker J. Palmer's writing explores how community is an integral aspect to a spiritual life. In *A Hidden Wholeness*, he discusses how a human being's internal soul must align with the work/role he does in the external world. He cautions us to carefully balance silence and solitude with dialogue and togetherness:

> Of course, solitude is essential to personal integration: there are places in the landscapes of our lives where no one can accompany us. But because we are communal creatures who need each other's support—and because, left to our own devices, we have an endless capacity for self-absorption and self-deception—community is equally essential to rejoining soul and role.[44]

You may already know the value of silence and solitude. You may already know how crucial it is to first find peace and ease within yourself before you can hope to impact the world. In this chapter, we will explore the value of finding and maintaining loving relationships with those who invigorate and inspire you further. As you dare to see relationships and desire differently—throwing off the mantle of identity labels and intentionally walking into the fires of jealousy—a new hunger will emerge in you for different kinds of relationships.

## Intentional Families

Practitioners of the polyamory movement teach about the importance of supporting, and being supported by, an *intentional family*. This type of family may include biological kin, but often it does not. (At this time on our planet, a majority of awakened people do not have blood relatives who are on a similar path.) The intentional family is the solution to a biological family that does not bring sufficient joy, inspiration, and unconditional love necessary for a life of intention.

The core of the intentional family—what glues it together—is a shared value system. While the specific value system differs from family to family, some common ones are: the sustainability/green movement, feminist and queer political work, holistic health practices, and shared interest in certain erotic adventures such as sacred sexuality or BDSM.

An intentional family is a flexible network of friends, lovers, partners, and their children, who come together to love, seek, and create their *own* traditions set apart from normative social conditioning. They eat meals together; they play together; they vacation together; they build businesses and create art together; they spend holidays together; they practice meditation and ritual together. Often, they share touch, sex, and physical pleasure. In a sense, the intentional family is the creative offspring of the commune movement of the 1960s and 1970s. Yet, its current form is different in two significant ways. Unlike communes, intentional families are often locationally dispersed—they do not always all live together on a single property. Also, there is now increased awareness about the flexibility of gender expression: Lovers in intentional families often choose partners based upon energetic, spiritual connections regardless of the shape or form of the body/ies concerned.

## Repression

Too often, people are surrounded by those who are *not* intentionally selected. Rather, too often, people are surrounded by those who seem to be there out of random chance or dire necessity.

A majority on this planet drag themselves daily to a job they hate, working with those who create an environment of negativity and suffering. A majority of people do *not* choose their friends wisely—instead, they "kill time" at bars and golf courses with people who they secretly find uninspiring, or even repulsive.

Why? Certainly, one answer is the fear of loneliness. People would rather spend time with *anyone*, rather than risk the potential solitude that might come from being more selective. Another answer is social pressure. There is pressure to interact with the people who want to interact with us—so if someone from our workplace or from our neighborhood asks us to spend time together, we feel as if we should say yes. We feel it is the polite or correct thing to do.

An intentional life is a life of choices—sometimes hard choices. When we wake up to the sheer miracle and ecstasy that is living life, that is being alive, we realize that life is too precious to waste on those who drain our energy. We realize that choosing intentional relationships is not being selfish, but rather it is self-care. And self-care is the only possible backbone for living a life of intention, a life that will spread love, like wildfire, throughout the world.

Thus, it is a paradox. One must *seem* selfish in order to selflessly move into compassionate love for others. And, through feeling and experiencing compassionate love, courage becomes the obvious, and actually only, choice.

## Beyond Closets

People who are gay, lesbian, bisexual, trans, queer, and polyamorous have learned a valuable lesson that is broadly applicable to anyone at the stage of spiritual growth where courage to find like-minded others becomes not a luxury but a necessity. This lesson is openness. As Deborah Anapol puts it: "closets are notoriously poor places to meet people."[45]

If you find yourself in a closet, if you realize that you've been keeping your desires secret, it is not necessary to bemoan that fact or to look back with regret. Closets are an understandable part of the journey! Closets keep us safe, allowing us the necessary time to mull over questions about what it is that we really want from life, and who it is we really are. In other words, a closet is like a waiting room: you are no longer on the outside (you now have some experience of a certain way of thinking and being), but you have not yet fully entered the place of your destination.

At a certain point, though, closets become stifling. There is no oxygen. There is darkness. Breath and light are needed. As we move toward what Parker J. Palmer calls an "undivided life," it becomes necessary to courageously reveal ourselves to others. When we finally do so, we then can more easily find others who have also made such revelations. We come together with those who understand.

Whether it is being open about our sexuality, our gender expression, our relationships, our passions, our artistic nature, or being open about our spiritual practices... whatever it is... it is crucial to eventually take that leap into openness. Only by revealing who we really are will we be able to connect with those loving companions who will take our evolution to new levels.

## Taking Action; Loosening Ties

There is the following truism in the polyamory community: *There may be unlimited love, but there is not unlimited time.* What this means is that even though the *idea* of having multiple romantic partnerships might sound wonderful in theory, one must balance the theory with the reality that there are only so many hours in a day. Just as choosing to give birth to one more child means more busyness and responsibility, having more partners and relationships means more busyness, more responsibility.

When you open the adventure of living a non-normative, intentional life—a life where love is seen as abundant rather than scarce—you will need to make choices. This equally applies whether you are poly or not. You will need to weigh the wonderful ideas you have versus the realities that are present. You have limited time as a being in this body; you will die one day. So... what will you do? How will you allocate your time? How will you follow the voice of desire? Who will be the people with whom you choose to spend the most time?

You may find that as you invest your energy in support systems, networks, and communities that bolster your spiritual growth, you will have less and less of an inclination to spend time with those whose paths are not as closely aligned with yours. While it is true that every human being you encounter has the potential to teach you important lessons, it is *also true* that being in a physical body automatically narrows down the amount of possible lessons you can learn in one lifetime. Thus, there are choices that need to be made.

Here is an example. Let's say you have a strong desire to move to Australia. You have an intuition that if you move there, many wonderful adventures would be in store, and much growth would occur. You know it, in your very bones. Yet, you *also* have a strong desire to move to Alaska. You have a feeling that were you to move there you would encounter situations and people that would help you evolve your consciousness. So, what to do? Because you are a human being, temporarily limited by time and space, you cannot live simultaneously in these two places. You must make a choice. You must pick one over the other, even though, in reality, both places would be wonderful.

No matter what choice you make, both options have *equal potential* to be wonderful because you have full authority over *yourself.* You have authority over your own emotional reactions and you have authority over the peace of mind you choose to cultivate. So, in a sense, the big choice you make about where to live matters less than the little mental-emotional choices you make daily after you have made the big choice. Will you second-guess or regret your choice, or will you simply be calm and content with the choice you have made? Will you worry, or will you be at peace? Will you stress or complain, or will you have gratitude?

Whether or not you choose to call your support network an intentional family, what you seek, at this point in your journey, will have the feeling of family. You will connect with those who want what you want: love, abundance, joy, compersion, adventure, desire, empathy, openness. As you feel the miracle of this intentional life, this kind of blessed unfolding, you may find that there are those from your past who no longer support you, and who you can no longer support in quite the same way. Sure, there is still love there—there always will be—yet you find you cannot invest the same kind of energy into those people, those places, those events, those traditions. Much of the old is falling away, and the new has arrived.

Many people are afraid of letting go of the old. Because of their fear, they remain stuck, motionless. Because of their fear, the voice of desire becomes more and more difficult to discern... and without a way to clearly discern desire, without a way to confidently chart their own path, waking up in the morning becomes a little less magical each morning. Life seems routine. Boring. Uninspired. This is the sad state of our planet, at this time. Many people would rather choose a (false) sense of security, certain with the familiar, than strike out into unknown territory. This is why so many people maintain intense connections with their biological families or with their friends from childhood—despite the fact that the energy that used to make those interactions feel worthwhile has long ago disintegrated.

The normal world may tell you that it is wrong to "betray" your old friends or "abandon" your family... and yet what could be more wrong than denying the voice of your innermost desire? What could feel more wrong than ignoring the fire inside of you that wants to embark on new adventures with new people who more succinctly align with your path of intention?

It may be, and probably will be, that as you open new ways of seeing love, embracing the worldview that love is abundant (rather than scarce), there will be people in your life who will fall away from you. They will leave you or you will leave them, or you will both leave each other. This is okay. This is the natural way, the way of change, the way of impermanence.

By recognizing and embracing the law of change, the law of impermanence, many polyamorous people have learned the lesson that a relationship can best be evaluated not by its longevity (which is the normative view), but rather by the quality of the relationship during the time of its happening. In other words, the time together does not matter as much as how much love was present. Therefore, if a relationship is no longer serving the best interests of everyone involved, then that relationship can be honored through a respectful and peaceful transition. In polyamorous lingo, the phrase "breaking up" is eschewed in favor of the term transitioning, because the former phrase automatically implies pain and trauma, while the latter term simply denotes change. (See Chapter 6 for more about the art of transitioning.)

When people transition, when people move apart from each other, when people—for various reasons—go their separate ways, what is the quality of that separation? If separation is done in the spirit of gratitude and love, then, ultimately, isn't that separation merely an extension of that loving relation? In this sense, a transition can be viewed not as a separation, but as a continuation into a different form. Indeed, the pain of change can be lessened, or even possibly eliminated, when we remember that we are all One. We will always be One. There really is no goodbye.

Even something as potentially difficult as a divorce can be done with grace. If you are going through such a situation, you can ask yourself: How can I be calm and present in this moment? How can I take responsibility for the choices I have made? What do I have to feel grateful for? How can I communicate clearly and with openness about how I am feeling and what I am thinking? How can I honor the marriage that was past, and the future that is unknown?

If people can undergo a transition with loving intent, then that relationship has been/is a successful one. In normative culture, the only relationships that are deemed successful are the ones that "last forever." But we must question this standard. In questioning, we notice that this criterion has been the insidious reason why so many people cling to passionless relationships. It's why people have affairs. A wise perspective does not judge a relationship by its duration; rather, a wise perspective under-stands that a relationship, regardless of its apparent duration, was/is a good one if the people can maintain loving intent towards each other. Is this easy? Often, no. The work can be difficult. Yet the rewards are beyond imagining. The rewards are letting go of the old ways of blame. You no longer have to blame the person or blame yourself when the time is right to transition.

To seek out a support network that inspires further evolution is not to pretend that those networks will never involve pain or suffering. "It is not that people won't betray you," Gangaji writes. "It is not that your heart won't break again and again. Opening to whatever is present can be a heartbreaking business. But let the heart break, for your breaking heart only reveals a core of love unbroken."[46]

∞

## Practice: Cord-cutting Ritual

As you invest your energy into people who can support you on your path, you may find you need to walk away from others. Whether it is your biological relatives or your coworkers or your best friend from seventh grade makes no difference. The realization that this person or those people are no longer boosting but rather draining your energy is not a judgment upon them, but rather it is simply a fact. That fact can be understood and felt without hatred, bitterness, or condemnation.

As you care for yourself, and as you open yourself to abundant love, you understand that those people from whom you walk away will have their choices to make, too. If they are angry or upset at you, that is not your burden to bear.

Although it may first appear a paradox, you can distance

yourself in a way that is filled with love. You can say move apart in a way that shows respect for the past shared experiences, while simultaneously respecting both you and them in the present.

A relationship must be beneficial for *all* involved. When that harmony is no longer manifest, a change must occur. Whether that change be a move to another continent, a switch from a marriage to a friendship, or perhaps even simply the choice to become online correspondents rather than meet in-person... the choice is a choice that can be done with love.

If there is a person in your life with whom you must make a more drastic separation, you can perform a cord-cutting ritual to help you achieve your intent of making the separation not a "break up," but rather a loving transition.

Find a quiet, peaceful place. Close your eyes. Take a few minutes to get in touch with your body through focusing your attention on your inhalations and exhalations. Simply feel the air moving into your nose, down into your lungs and belly, and then coming up again through your nose. Sit with those sensations for awhile.

When you are ready, imagine there is a cord connecting you to the person with whom you'd like to separate. (If there are multiple people from whom you need to separate, repeat this ritual for each person.) The cord connects your navel to the other person's navel. Allow the cord to be whatever color feels right to you—the color can be purple, silver, gold, white, black, or whatever color enters your mind. Take a few minutes to simply see the cord and see you connected to that person. Breathe in and out, seeing and feeling that connection.

As you are ready, visualize a pair of scissors cutting that cord. As you make the cut, allow any emotions that need to arise, arise. You may suddenly find yourself crying. You may find that you scream or yell or groan. Make any noises or movements that feel necessary—hold nothing back. After the cord has been cut, see the person receding, away from you. They may be walking, floating, flying, or running. Allow the departure.

Return to your breathing. When it feels right, open your eyes. Say a few words of gratitude to yourself. Thank yourself for having the courage to perform this ritual.

## The Future

As you move into the future, allow your actions to support the ritual you have just completed and allow your actions to further invest in the community you need. Volunteer your time: do small things like wash dishes, give backrubs, or meet with those going through difficult times. Be there for them, as they are there for you. You will be amazed at how clearly, now, the voice of desire comes, and how quickly and effortlessly you will be able to interpret it. Life is becoming more beautiful.

As you bond with your new community, you will find the courage within to take on a very important step in your journey—the time of forgiveness and healing. This is a time of letting go of the past. This is a time of dropping the burden you've been hauling around. It's a time for courage; it's a time for sheer trust that the universe is a loving universe. It's time for dropping blame, dropping the ego, and dropping pain.

# Chapter 6

# Healing and Forgiveness

*Wholeness or healing spreads through all your relationships like a light that makes the world warmer and kinder for everyone. In other words, by healing yourself, you heal everyone around you.*
—Stephen Russell[47]

*If you have wondered what you are doing on this planet, now your question has been answered. You, dear one, are here to forgive. Whatever has happened in your life has occurred to support you in learning this one lesson. Each player upon the stage of your life's drama that has upset you in any way came into the play at your subconscious request, to give you the opportunity to learn the lesson of forgiveness.*
—Joan Gattuso[48]

## Intentionality and Healing

To evolve one's consciousness is to transform. It is the process of the dry dead tree in winter becoming an abundant flowering beauty of the spring. To evolve, to grow, to awaken, to become spiritually enlightened—these are all terms for the same process of transformation. These are all ways to describe moving out of the past and into the present moment.

When transformation happens, deep healing happens on emotional, physical, mental, and spiritual levels. Healing is something everyone needs—no one is exempt. Even His Holiness the Dalai Lama has said that his aim is to heal himself, through forgiving the Chinese, who have violently occupied his Tibetan homeland. Even the Dalai Lama has to heal.

Transformation and healing are interdependent processes. Simply put: One does not heal without one's life changing dramatically. This is the reason why healing can seem so elusive. People intuitively realize (sometimes consciously, sometimes not) that to heal quite literally means to transform—and to transform means change. Change is often unwelcome. People fear change; people fear what does not seem stable, secure, and predictable. Therefore, many people who want healing are not healed (or only partially healed), because there is a part of their psyche that fears the big changes that are an intrinsic part of the healing process.

Indeed, to undergo healing requires courage; it is not, by nature, an effortless or easy process. Healing does not just spontaneously happen to the "lucky"—nay, healing is an act of intention. It takes growing pains. If we see that it is the nature of the universe to grow, to evolve, then we can see that *healing is at the core of life itself.* To heal is to evolve.

Without intentionally embracing a healing path, a path of evolution, one feels as though life is stagnant. Robotic. Frustrating. Even terrifying. Without healing, the wounds of the past combine with the stressors of the present, and we find ourselves sitting in a bathtub overflowing with thick toxic black sludge. The process of healing begins with the intention to simply open the drain—let it go. Then, forgiveness is to refill that bathtub with the light of acceptance and unconditional love.

Of course, if you are intending to cure yourself of a physical illness, you will want to take steps to help your body heal. You may switch to an organic or vegetarian diet, you may begin an exercise program, you may move to a climate that is more hospitable, you may avoid chemicals in your household products, you may avoid alcohol and caffeine... these are good steps to take. All these actions will be tools to help your body recover. Yet, if you do not practice forgiveness, you will be perpetually reaching—and not finding—a lasting state of balance. The diet and the exercise and the other physical practices can only do so much. To heal, you will need to go deeper.

As your relationships deepen with compassion and unconditional love, and as you find more and more joy in your intentional relationships and intentional communities, it will become clear that forgiveness and healing are the next step on your journey. Even the tiniest remnants of bitterness, resentment, judgment, or anger will begin to feel like huge thorns in your heart.

The time has come to heal. The time has come to forgive.

## Healing and the Past

Each moment, each person is presented with an ever-renewing choice: either *be* in the present moment, or lug around the past. If we choose to lug around the past, we are choosing to drain our vital life force because the past is where the ego loves to dwell. (The ego is the part of us that forgets that we are interconnected with all beings.) The ego gets a kick out of rehashing what others "should have done" and what "mistakes" we made. The ego loves to harshly judge others and self—and the past is a massive resource for such a game.

As you explore alternative ways of enjoying intimate relationships that satisfy your own voice of desire rather than the social pressure of what's considered normal, you may suddenly, and perhaps confusingly, find that thinking of the past has become a burden. You have changed so much already, and when you think back to your past relationships you can now perceive the dysfunction in them. The mere thought of a promise you made but broke, or a relationship you loved but lost, may be enough to bring you to tears. You may begin to dwell on the conflicts, problems, miscommunications, or deceits from the past, and become overly anxious about avoiding these "mistakes" in the future. This chapter is for those who find themselves at such a crossroads.

## No Mistakes

Before we can delve into the philosophy and practice of forgiveness, it will be helpful to clear away a mental formation that may be weighing us down. The word *mistake* is one of the greatest confusions created by the fearful ego. As the ego is the part of us that does not recognize the interconnectedness of all beings, then it makes sense that the ego would create the idea of a mistake. A mistake is a sense of separation from what is, and from what "might have been" or "should have been." Mistake is the realm of regret; mistake is the realm of the ego.

There is no such thing as a mistake. Every person we interact with and every situation in our life is absolutely the right person, the right situation, the right time. *There is no exception to this.* Holding the mental formation that there can be a mistake—that there can be a "bad" choice or a "good" choice—is a thought that creates fear and anxiety.

Every human being wants to do what they consider the good choice, the right choice. However, we have been socially conditioned to think otherwise. Our mainstream values have insisted that there are lazy people, sneaky people, corrupt people, and intrinsically evil people. But this is not so. At the core of everyone and everything is the seed of love and the desire to grow and transform. Sure, some people may, by the choices they make, take a longer time getting there—but, in the end, everyone either inches or sprints in the same direction, the direction of love.

Even a person who commits suicide believes they are making a good choice, or else they would not do it. Why would they go through the potential physical pain unless they believed it was a good choice to make? Likewise, a person who commits murder also believes in the rightness of their action, or else they would not do it. Everything a human being does is done because they believe, in that moment, that it is the right thing to do—"right" meaning the course of action that is the best possible one for that place/time and under those particular circumstances. And even if they perceive that there are no other options than the one they must take, then that lack of options is the reality upon which they make their choice—a choice they will always perceive as right.

If all human beings make choices that they believe are right, then what is the point of harboring negative emotions towards a person or situation? To approach life with the mentality that it is possible to make a mistake causes needless suffering. Instead, we can replace that mentality with the calm assurance that everything that happens, every choice we make, is the right happening, the right choice. Everything that happens, every life circumstance, is the result of a loving universe. This is not some New Age feel-good-mumbo-jumbo. This is the reality of how the universe works.

∞

## Practice: Feeling the Flow

There are times in our lives when we can second-guess or regret a choice. When this happens, our emotions are pulled into a whirlwind of anxiety, tension, confusion, and sorrow.

In this simple and ancient practice of using light to heal, we learn to feel, in our bodies, the very and absolute rightness of the universe. We feel the flow of love, which dissolves all insecurities and reminds us that everyone and everything is connected—so there is no reason to fear that a mistake has been, or ever will be made.

Find a calm, private place where you will not be interrupted. Sit in a comfortable position. Take some cleansing breaths. Visualize light entering your crown. You can picture this light as a single column of light or as rays of the sun. As you feel the light entering your crown, allow that light to continue travelling down your body, entering your face, neck, heart, belly, and all the way down to your toes.

Allow the light to cleanse you of fear and worry. Continue to simply absorb the light, feeling it in every cell of your body, feeling it assure you that you are on the right path—you have always been on the right path. There is no reason to fear. Allow the light to glue you to the present moment, and as you inhale and exhale feel the love and the absolute rightness that permeates all.

## Defining Forgiveness

People often define forgiveness in ways that cause needless anxiety. Forgiveness doesn't mean we have to forget. Forgiveness doesn't mean we have to enjoy spending time with the person(s) who were involved in the hurt. Forgiveness doesn't mean we have to ask God or some authority figure for pardon.

Forgiveness is simple: It's about letting go. It's about living in the present moment with a calm trust that the universe is a universe of love. As Caroline Myss sums it up: "Forgiving does not mean saying that what happened to you doesn't matter, or that it is all right for someone to have violated you. It simply means releasing the negative feelings you have about that event and the person or persons involved."[49] If we approach forgiveness in this way, we see that forgiveness (healing) is a choice we make *for our own well-being*—and, further, the person(s) we forgive do not necessarily even have to know that we forgave them. Forgiveness is an act of and for the self.

∞

## Practice: Speaking Forgiveness

This practice of healing and forgiveness does not require talking to a therapist (although that can help) or undergoing lengthy training with a master. This is a simple process that requires no money, no previous training, and it can be done in the comfort of your own home, at your own pace.

Find a quiet place in your home where you will not be interrupted. It will be helpful if you choose a place that feels very safe to you. For me, that place is soaking in the bathtub, with the lights turned off and candles or sage burning. Find your own special place.

Turn off your phone and all gadgets. Lock the door. Notify your partner(s) or roommate(s) ahead of time that they may hear all sorts of noises, such as talking, crying, or even yelling/shouting emanating from the room, and that you would like to be left undisturbed until you emerge. Make sure they understand that this practice is something wonderful for you — and not something they should worry about. If you live in an apartment, it would be helpful to have an object that may help to muffle any loud sounds, such as a pillow.

It is important that you carry out this practice on a day where you have many consecutive hours at your disposal. The ideal situation would be to begin in the morning or early afternoon of a day that you have only relaxation and/or spiritual practice as the intention for the entire day. In other words, give yourself no restrictions regarding time, except for holding the intention that you will conclude the practice before you go to sleep that night.

After you settle into your safe space, take a few moments to breathe. Feel your belly, as it rises and falls with each inhale and exhale. As you are ready, begin to speak aloud to the person and/or situation that you need to forgive. Address the parties by name, and feel that they can hear you.

Begin by saying aloud your intention to move into the present, and no longer lug around the baggage of the past. Then, tell the story out loud. Start at the beginning. If, for example, you need to heal from a divorce, tell the story of the relationship from the beginning. Tell of how you met, how you fell in love, every detail that comes to mind. Then progress to where you are now, at the point of needing to forgive.

As you speak, remember that it is just you in the room, so

there is no need to censor yourself. You probably will sigh, cry, moan, and you may even start feeling nauseous. If you feel nausea coming on, you can release this feeling by letting out a primal scream. It may feel strange or somehow dangerous or risky to do so (and it definitely goes against so-called proper "polite" etiquette!), but if you can expel all the pent-up frustration and other toxic emotions from your being through screaming, you will feel immediate relief.

Speak speak speak until you come to the point where there is nothing left to say about that person and/or situation. Cry cry cry until you come to the point where there is nothing left to cry about. It may take minutes, or it may take hours. You will know when that point comes.

If you devote yourself to this practice, you will see the positive results in your life and you may begin to then realize that you can release hurt *as it happens,* and not have to wait months or years to perform the release in such a dramatic way. If you feel hurt, if you feel anger, if you feel sorrow, if you feel any negative emotion, you don't have to wait until later. After you have performed the forgiveness practice once or a few times, your system will be cleaner, so you may find that you do not want to let any of the toxic sludge build up again. Practice forgiveness on a daily basis, *as events arise.* When you realize you are holding negative feelings toward a person or situation, immediately (or as soon as you can) stop what you are doing, close your eyes, and breathe, releasing the toxicity from your system and reminding yourself that what is happening is not a mistake.

Making forgiveness a part of your regular spiritual practice will connect you further to your voice of desire. Forgiveness will give you a deep sense of peace, and also direction. You know that any person or event that you encounter does not have the power to drain you. You can accept people and situations uncondi-tionally.

## Transitioning and the Art of Acceptance

The Vietnamese Buddhist monk Thich Nhat Hanh writes prolifically on the two related practices of compassion and forgiveness. Many of his teachings center on his experiences at Plum Village, the monastery in France where he makes his home. He emphasizes the necessity of forgiveness as being essential to maintaining healthy relationships. "People who lack compassion, love, and forgiveness suffer a lot," he writes. "When you can forgive, when you can accept, you feel light, and you can relate to other living beings. Without compassion, you are utterly alone. That is why compassion is the ground of happiness."[50]

If we can feel compassion, if we can forgive, we can live peacefully and productively in the social world. Without these, we are ruled by the destructive power of the ego — the ego that nags at us to dislike, criticize, hate, or even seek revenge.

The healing power of forgiveness, however, is challenging to learn because it is not taught in our normative culture. What is considered normal is to hold grudges. What is considered normal is to feel self-righteous and to put others down. What is considered normal is to defend ourselves from the so-called "attacks" of those who do not do what we would like in the exact way that we would like it. On a larger scale, this is the reason for wars and civil unrest.

In the polyamory movement, there is a concept known as *transitioning*. This term replaces the culturally normative concept of "breaking up." The concept of transitioning acknowledges that people change and circumstances change. To practice the art of transitioning is to release the typical urge to attack or blame, because there is nothing that is broken. Instead of thinking in terms of breaking up, it is simply acknowledged that a relationship is changing its form. A marriage may transition to co-parenting; a live-in relationship may transition to a long-distance relationship; a girlfriend may transition to a lover; a boyfriend may transition to a dating companion; a primary partner may transition to a secondary partner; a spouse may transition to a friend. The possibilities are infinite. It all depends on the people involved and the new labels and arrangements that everyone agrees to.

Transitioning can also describe the grey area when a relationship is changing, but there is not yet an understanding of what the parties need or want. Those who practice polyamory understand, perhaps better than most, that intimate relationships, like life, are constantly in flux. Relationships are dynamic. They move and shift as people move and shift. It brings great suffering to expect a relationship to continue "forever" in a certain way. Even if a relationship is maintained, for example, between two people over the course of a lifetime (a very rare occurrence), those two people—as time passes—will undergo many radical upheavals, transformations, and situations that will totally change the way they perceive themselves, as well as the way they perceive each other and the relationship.

Every relationship, regardless of the number of people involved, is always by nature an impermanent form—for it can never stay static; it is always in motion. Therefore, it is wise to assess the quality of a relationship not by its duration or its ability to last a lifetime; rather it is wise to assess a relationship by asking: Were/are the people in the relationship honest with each other? Were/are the people in the relationship loving and compassionate toward each other? Too often, in normative culture, the only yardstick we have to assess whether a relationship is successful is whether or not it lasts a lifetime. This sort of thinking does not take into account the law of impermanence. Much suffering is a result.

Some relationships last decades; others last days. Some relationships seem, at the beginning, as though they will be quite durable—but then, unexpected circumstances happen, causing people to evolve and move in different directions. There is no shame in this. There is no shame in change! To move away from a person/relationship does *not* signal failure.

Indeed, to bemoan change is painful. It unnecessarily drains one's energy. To actively embrace change as not only an inescapable part of relating *but also as the very stuff of life* is to remove a great deal of pressure from a relationship. If we embrace the reality of impermanence, we shift the focus to honesty and cultivating authenticity, rather than feeling we must stay together in the same way for all time. We can focus on unconditional love, rather than feeling we must change our loved one. We can focus on forgiveness.

## Andrew and Anya: The "Divorce"

It is most fateful to be writing about forgiveness at this time in my life. Just yesterday, Andrew and I visited the county court-house to have our marriage dissolved. It was interesting and rather surreal to sit in the waiting room, receiving sympathetic glances from officials and other citizens who believed that our divorce must be a sad thing. We probably were one of the few couples to ever enter those domestic relations courthouse doors with lightness in our hearts, holding hands. After our "divorce," we spent the afternoon cuddling on the couch, laughing, kissing, reminiscing about the past, and speaking hopeful words.

In truth, this was not the end of our relationship, rather it was a legal choice we both made, based upon a number of factors, the greatest of which was that Andrew no longer felt comfortable being legally married to me (or anyone), because he could not *also* legally marry his other life partner Cordelia. For Andrew, the fact that he could not also marry his other great love irked him to the point where a legal end to our marriage seemed the only way of protesting a broken system, a system that fails to recognize the potential beautiful diversity of family.

Looking back, it does not surprise me that this happened. On the day we were wed, we already felt a huge amount of guilt at even doing so, because we recognized that in the state in which we lived (Michigan), our gay, lesbian, bisexual, and other queer friends could not enjoy the same privilege we did. We found it problematic that the only qualification for our marriage was the fact that he had a penis and I had a vagina. At the time, we attempted to assuage our guilt by making a political speech during the ceremony, in an effort, as we said, "to clear our conscience while also raising some consciousness."

Despite our uncomfortable feelings, though, we did get married and we did enjoy the social privileges and recognition that marriage brought to our relationship. After about five years, however, Andrew and I became uncomfortable with not only the sex requirement of marriage in our state (only male and female may marry), but also the number requirement. Just as Andrew couldn't marry Cordelia under the current legal system, Cordelia would not be able to marry Mark if she wanted to, nor I with Robert. Time passed, our poly relationships deepening, and we began to see marriage as something that did not accurately describe the reality of our day-to-day lives.

Getting married is not something Andrew and I regret. Nor do we criticize those who seek marriage or enjoy their current marriage. Marriage can be a beautiful, wonderful public celebration! Andrew and I desired that wedding ceremony as a way to kick off our long-term journey together. Truly, that day was magical. The energy offered from our loved ones on that summer day, July 2008, was a tremendous gift. We still regularly bathe ourselves in memories of that day. In fact, sometimes when I have difficulty falling asleep, I think of our wedding day, and my body can then relax into a happy slumber.

No mistakes; no regrets.

## Andrew and Anya: Sorrow and Confusion

A few years ago, when Andrew first broached the topic of divorce, I took it personally. I took it hard. I mistakenly believed he no longer loved me. In my heart and mind, I associated the word divorce, as most people do, with darkness. Divorce as failure. Divorce as sorrow. Divorce as regret. Consequently, we went through many months of tears and confusion, as Andrew repeatedly stated that his love for me had *not* diminished, and that getting a legal divorce would actually be in sync with what we daily professed as polyamory teachers: love as abundant, love as dynamic, love beyond labels, love beyond gender or number.

However, for a long period of time I could not reconcile his suggestion of divorce with the normative cultural values that had been blazed onto my heart since I was a child. The conditioning went deep. I was so angry at Andrew! What right did he have to suggest we no longer be married, if he truly still loved me?

I initially did not want to give up the social status that marriage accorded, even if doing so would indeed align with Andrew's and my ethics. As months passed, my fears and anxieties about our relationship accumulated. My health suffered. I began to snap at Andrew, criticizing him for the smallest of details. I found myself jealous of Cordelia for the first time in a long time. I found it hard to concentrate, and many days I could not provide Reiki treatments for others because I felt that my light had become too diminished by fear and dread to be able to effectively heal another. It was an excruciating time, all because I was stubbornly clinging to the past picture of our relationship, to the past vision of who we used to be. In my confusion and sorrow, I was refusing to acknowledge that Andrew and Anya were changing.

## Andrew and Anya: Healing and Forgiveness
Finally, after months of suffering, I cleared an entire day in my schedule to get down to the hard work of forgiving us both. On a cloudy June afternoon, I sat in my bathtub and vowed not to come out until I had forgiven.

I needed to forgive myself, first, for clinging to the past picture of who we were at the time we got married. The truth is,

I loved those people! I loved their sense of youthful optimism and excitement. But, I had to let those people go. *Andrew and I were no longer those people.* We no longer believed that we were each other's "best and only," as we had expressed in those wedding vows. We loved other people. Andrew loved Cordelia and I loved Robert. And these new loves were amazing! These new loves brought such light: with the light multiplied between us all, bouncing back and forth, gaining speed with each day and with each new experience. We were finding, through polyamory, that we no longer had to fear jealousy—and, that we could actually feel happiness when our partner loved another. What a revelation! What a process of awesome and intense growth!

Andrew and I had discovered, through intense trial and error, that polyamory was not just about enjoying physical sex with multiple partners. Polyamory is about discovering a deep and lasting faith in the power of love, in love's abundance. We found our hearts open.

In order to truly live an intentional life, I realized I had to move forward with Andrew's request to end the legal marriage and I had to forgive myself for resisting it. And I had to forgive Andrew for changing—in other words, I had to release the toxic emotions I had carried, emotions that feared that if I lost the label "wife" I no longer lived in the core of his heart. I had to heal. I had to cut the cords to the past, and fully enter the present moment, with no restrictions, no baggage.

When I climbed out of the tub and unlocked the bathroom door, I noticed my body felt different. It was as though there had been a fist squeezed around my heart for months—and now, finally, my heart was free. The fist had dissolved. A few hours later, a dear friend phoned. She mentioned something about Andrew, and for the first time in many months, I found myself speaking of him with a smile.

## Moving into Magic

Whether polyamorous or monogamous or somewhere in between, it is imperative to relax into the reality that relationships and people change over time. Even though fear may sometimes arise, if we can practice forgiveness, if we can learn to stop dragging around the past, we can move into the present moment—a place of sheer magic, a place where all the typical rules of living no longer apply.

Moving into magic, we realize, perhaps for the first time, our own immense power. We begin to experiment. We thrill! We understand we are not special or gifted, but that our power comes, simply, as a natural extension of being alive. We understand ourselves as a being of light: as an inexhaustible conduit for creativity, and love. And we practice our relationships accordingly.

# Chapter 7

# Magical Relationships

*Every human is a magician.*
—Don Miguel Ruiz[51]

*The visible, outer world of form and appearance, the arena and stage upon which we collectively play out the human drama, is a metaphor for the invisible, inner realm. Thus we physically conduct formalized rituals in the visible realm to represent otherwise inexplicable metaphysical processes occurring in the invisible realm.*[52]
—Stephen Russell

If you had asked me, back before I began to love Rebecca, if my relationship with Andrew could be more wonderful, more lovely, more magical, I would have replied *no*. I would have said that he and I were joined together in bliss—and what could possibly be better than bliss?

The fact is, though, our relationship did deepen and transform into something even more magical than when it began. For when I sat with Andrew on that couch, that summer dawn, telling him I loved Rebecca, I was terrified.

Andrew's compassionate response amazed me. Kissing my forehead, he whispered encouragement, saying he would support whatever course of action I wanted to take. He assured me our love was strong. He reminded me of our wedding vows, of our promise to be honest with each other. Before drifting off to sleep that morning in his warm broad arms, he thanked me for my courage.

## Time's Guidebook

Certainly not every moment in Andrew's and my relationship has been as beautifully cinematic as that morning on the couch. Just like any human relationship, we have had our issues, dramas, and problems. We have even had moments where we questioned whether the passion we shared was drawing to a close. Yet, we carry the spirit of that morning—where we both opened to a deeper love through mutual honesty and courage—even today. We say we will carry it as long as we live. That is our promise to each other. Andrew and I carry the memory of that courageous, intentional morning, along with all the other countless moments where we made the choice, through the foundation of honesty, to foster an intentional relationship.

Since that summer morning, we have experienced the comings and goings of his lovers and my lovers. We have experienced the shaping of our ethics and dreams by the ethics and dreams of those we befriend and with whom we make committed partnerships. Andrew and I continue to change. Our relationship continues to change. We are not the people we were when we got married. It is tempting, sometimes, to flip through photo albums, to feel nostalgic for the time when it was "just us." But it is important we do not dwell on the past. Impermanence, the law of living in time, is our guidebook for how to live love. We continue to watch with amazement as we each grow and open further, and we remember to have patience and practice unconditional love when the other person stumbles or behaves in a way that does not appear ideal.

In truth, though, we know that all actions *are* ideal—because there can be no mistakes. Both through the daily mundane and through those dramatic, cinematic moments we have learned what it means to love and what it means to move through Earthly Time intensely connected to another soul. Even though we enjoy other intimate relationships, our dynamic is, ultimately, the dynamic between the two of us: Andrew and Anya. It is only us, him and me, who decide what our relationship is and will be. In that way, our relationship is no different from a monogamous one. Though our universe is inhabited by constellations of other loving partners, friends, and intimates, we remember to cultivate the bond we share, knowing it does take effort, knowing it is up to us and only us to maintain our intention of honesty and courage.

And just as the love between Andrew and I is magic, so is my partnership with Robert, the man I currently share a home with. Robert and I walk side-by-side through life: we are a fiery team indeed, bonded together in a shared quest to create and experience beauty. When we play in the kitchen, we laugh, chop, sing, kiss... and, later, when we feast, our tongues delight in the infinite spice of being. Robert and I love passionately. As we wake in each other's arms, every inhale is gratitude; every exhale is curiosity—what will we learn next? Our lovemaking is meditation. Our orgasm is prayer.

All the love in my life that I choose to intentionally cultivate is magic. And not in a shallow Hallmark or Disney sense... I mean *actual magic*. As a human being, I know I am powerful and can create my life in the manner of my very dreaming. Life is magic, relationships are magic, everything I touch is magic. Anything is possible, given my mind and my partners' minds and hearts are focused on whatever intention we set.

My partners and I live courageously; we live queerly; we live so often against the dictates of the norm. Although others mock us or believe us to be naïve fools or judge us to be downright sinful, we strive to create our lives as we desire them.

How do we do this? How do we live this way? A major aspect of transforming desire into day-to-day reality is through our practice. One way to manifest magical relationships is through creating rituals.

## A Brief Note to Magic/Magick Practitioners

I realize that many of my readers will already be familiar with the practice of magic, such as those from the Pagan/Neopagan/Wicca communities, for example. Indeed, those of you who understand magic may have more experience than I.

This chapter is meant to explain magical practice at an introductory level. Yet, I have tried to make this chapter meaningful and useful, no matter your level of experience. It is my intention to offer both seasoned practitioners, as well as those completely new to magic, insights about how intentional relationships can be strengthened through living a life of magic.

## Magic and Ritual

When most people hear the word *magic*, they usually call to mind entertainment: David Copperfield, David Blaine, exotic-looking men in sparkling jumpsuits pulling rabbits out of hats or sawing a shrieking woman in half. They think of magic as only the stuff of dazzle, illusion, legend, folklore, myth. They think of magic only as a practiced sleight of hand, as the realm of fantasy only: not the stuff of real life. Indeed, magic—typically reserved for children, Christmas, or crazy people—tends not to be a serious subject of discussion in mainstream cultural dialogue. Yet, magic, often dismissed as make-believe, is a real and deep resource for creating an intentional, love-filled life.

Each of us carries an immense indwelling of power and possibility—and the only thing preventing us from utilizing that power and from realizing that possibility is our own ignorance of what we can do. It is as if most human beings live their entire lives as caterpillars, forever struggling along the ground—when they could begin, at any time, the process of transformation. We are not meant to stay caterpillars: we are meant take flight, diving and soaring by the grace of our own beautiful wings.

Why don't most people realize what they truly are? What incredible things they can do?

The answer to this question is complex, yet I believe it can be boiled down to a general explanation. *People forget that the physical world is not the only world.* In addition to the physical world, there is an unseen world—the world of energy. This world of energy, both mysterious and ineffable, interacts and overlaps with the physical world. Mystics and shamans have long understood this. Spiritual paths such as Taoism, Buddhism, Hinduism, Gnosticism, as well as all the various indigenous traditions, offer a way to bring together the forces of the unseen world and the seen world. That way is ritual.

There have been countless definitions of ritual offered throughout the ages. The definition I offer my clients and students is this: *Ritual is focused energetic intention achieved through physical practice.*

Notice this definition does not require you be a minister, master, or bearded yogi. Using ritual, anyone can do magic who has the willingness to do magic. In that sense, you could say that magic is actually mundane, because it is open to all, not exclusive to any person or group. Anyone can practice. Magic is simply the use of physical practice (ritual) designed to bring about a certain intention.

You might notice, too, that this definition of magic can also serve as the definition of meditation as well. Indeed: meditation, like magical ritual, is all about focused intention through physical acts, such as breathing, sitting, walking, etc. A person can meditate while being totally in the moment while gardening, washing dishes, or making love. Being in touch with the moment, and not allowing the mind to get carried away with thoughts, is the basis of meditation, and also magical ritual.

Ritual strengthens our feeling of connection to the cosmos. When we undergo ritual, we open ourselves to change, to be changed. And that kind of trust creates a chain reaction in our lives: we are given increasing amounts of power. If we make loving choices, our powers will increase. If we make choices out of fear or greed, then our powers will plateau, and eventually diminish, as our lives begin to feel, quite literally, out of our control.

Ritual is paradoxical. On the one hand, a ritual is performed to manifest some aspect of our psyche or our physical lives that we desire. So, in that sense, a ritual is used to assert our own powerful control over our lives. Yet, on the other hand, ritual is about letting go. Ritual is, in essence, saying to the universe: *Do with me as you please; I am your servant.*

As you can see, ritual is complicated. Even the great shamans and gurus will tell you their logical minds do not fully comprehend how ritual works. They will only tell you that it does work.

## Doing and Being Ritual

Ritual is about doing, while simultaneously being. In other words, we must clear our minds and intensely *be* in the present moment in order to perform an effective ritual. The converse is also true: while doing ritual, our minds can more naturally clear and we find ourselves immersed in the present moment of pure being-ness.

Consciousness evolves through doing ritual. (It must be said, however, that there are many ways to evolve consciousness, and this is merely one of the ways, not the *only* way.) Through ritual, our consciousness becomes increasingly more aware of itself *as consciousness*—and because consciousness *is* the entire universe, consciousness sees that it is immensely powerful. No longer the slugging caterpillar, but the rising butterfly. We realize magic is real. We feel our inborn ability to do it.

As we increasingly understand that love is abundant, and co-create relationships that correspond with that understanding, we realize our relationships will be what and how we intend. It's that simple. So, the question we must ask ourselves is very basic: *How do I want my relationships to be?*

# Joy

Probably the most profound teaching I have come across in my life came to me during ritual. Assisted by a mentor, I learned how to communicate with a sacred plant. After anointing my body with oil, she began to beat her drums, singing a song of ancient words. I entered a deep trance. Through the physical actions of oil, drum, and song, she opened a very precious time and space for me to perceive something that had already been there, yet I had not been able to perceive it before (due to my indoctrination in the normal world, the world where magic is not possible). Through her use of magical ritual, it became possible for me to move out of my ordinary ways of thinking, my ordinary mind patterns, and thus perceive the plant in a new way, allowing me to communicate with it in words.

During our ritual, the plant conveyed to me a teaching that changed my life forever. The plant spoke to me in a gentle, balanced tone. The teaching was this:

*Do the things that make you feel joyful. Conversely, do not do the things that do not make you feel joyful. Therefore, when an idea comes into your mind that brightens and lifts your heart, you should do this good idea. If an idea comes into your mind that brings you sadness or anxiety, then do not carry out this idea.*

This message has helped me on numerous occasions where I second-guessed my intuition or when I had a difficult time hearing what my gut had to say. My life became much simpler. I have a guidepost now that helps me cut through the clutter, slow down, and hear my own voice of desire. I now aim to do only that which makes me feel joyful (if not in that moment, then in the long run, as a result of an action or series of actions). If I have a thought that seems like something I "should" do, but the thought makes me feel sad or anxious, then no matter how logically sound the idea appears to be, it is not something I put into practice. Perhaps in the future the timing might be right for that idea, but not now. There have been times, of course, when I have experienced sadness or difficult emotions as I have intentionally entered a trial or an ordeal, but I have always been able to perceive the joyful core at the center of the sadness. If I cannot perceive that joyful core, then I know I am on the wrong path, and know it is time to change directions.

As we answer the question of how you want your relationships to be (truly a lifelong question, the answer of which must be continually revised over time as wisdom deepens), we may find ourselves asking a parallel question: *What brings me joy?* If we understand what it is that brings us joy, we can then cultivate relationships that bring and sustain joy.

Your understanding of joy may be different than the one I understand. Reflect for yourself. How do you define joy? Reflecting upon and understanding what will bring joy is crucial in answering the question of how we want our relationships to be.

## Immanence

As you ask yourself these important questions, also ask yourself about your relationship to/with all people, all beings, and all of life. The concept of *immanence*, stemming from the ancient Goddess traditions, reminds us of this sacredness. Immanence means that divinity is not up in the sky or relegated to some remote kingdom, but rather divinity is embodied here and now in every single being—from our lovers to our neighbors to the strangers across the ocean to the ants crawling up the trees in our backyard. As Starhawk puts it in her book, *The Spiral Dance*, immanence reminds us that "we are each a manifestation of the living being of earth" and "that nature, culture, and life in all their diversity are sacred. Immanence calls us to live our spirituality here in the world, to take action to preserve the life of the Earth, to live with integrity and responsibility."[53]

If we are guided by the teaching of immanence, we can then perceive all our social interactions as sacred, since we all are—no matter our history, race, social class, or background—sacred beings. Each moment of being in the presence of a being is sacred!

Therefore, doing ritual is about embodying the sacredness that is already present in all of life. And ritual is about celebration, because it allows us to feel what is already there: sacredness in every cell, every whisper, every tree, every robin's song. Every. All.

Ritual is a way of re-training your mind in the ancient wisdom of sacredness. This is not taught in our mainstream culture. What we are taught is that life is cheap, relationships are disposable, and that our power resides in what we purchase at the store. Our normal society promotes these dark, shallow, depressing values.

Through ritual, we begin to realize that life does not have to be the way we were taught. Life can be, as Don Miguel Ruiz teaches, a kind of heaven on Earth:

I want you to forget everything you have learned in your whole life. This is the beginning of a new understanding, a new dream. The dream you are living is your creation. It is your perception of reality that you can change at any time. You have the power to create hell, and you have the power to create heaven. Why not dream a different dream? Why not use your mind, your imagination, and your emotions to dream heaven?[54]

As we discover how we want our relationships to be, and as we discover what brings us joy, we can begin to dream a new dream. We can begin to live in a magical world inhabited by beings who are just as beautiful and sacred as we are. Every time we come into contact with them, we are curious and then we learn from them. As we embody the principle of immanence, we begin to heal wounds, and—through that healing—we begin to imagine life in a lighter way. No longer do we lug around the baggage instilled in us from our confused, dark culture—we are free to step lightly and enthusiastically, in a true heaven on Earth. Through experimenting with rituals others teach us, and also by inventing our own, we learn to trust ourselves, and as we trust ourselves we raise our consciousness. We evolve. And, we delight in the fact that we cannot predict who we are becoming. The road ahead is unknown, and we are not afraid.

In the next pages, I will provide some examples of magical rituals you can begin to practice. Please be aware that magic will still work even if you have some doubts. So, even if you do not fully feel yourself as the butterfly yet, trust that the process of evolving consciousness is already in motion. Have patience with yourself, and watch the wonderfulness unfold. As you set your intentions and practice magic, be prepared for the external conditions and circumstances of your life to change, such as relationships, jobs, or the location of your home. Massive rearrangements of your life *will happen*, because magic works by shifting the preexisting elements of your life so that there can be the space necessary for your intention to manifest. Simply put, the old needs to be shaken up, to pave the way for the new. Keeping in mind the law of impermanence helps to bring comfort in confusing times of rapid change.

Most importantly, remember this: *The universe will grant what you ask for.* It may not happen on your ideal timeline, and the rearrangements of your life required to manifest the request may be a total surprise, but it *will* come. Therefore, be as specific as possible when you craft your intention(s) for each ritual. Ask yourself what you really want, and be prepared for the inevitable change required in your life for the intention to manifest into being. Be open. Be ready. Fill your heart with love. And breathe.

∞

## Rituals: Magic of the Self

The basic elements of performing a magical ritual are twofold: the act of setting an intention (what you wish to manifest), and the utilization of tools. The tools can be items from nature such as stones, water, fire, flowers, or the tools can be as simple as your breath, your hands, or your own silence.

Indeed, magical ritual need not be intricate or overly complicated. In fact, you may already be practicing magic. Do you pray? Do you seek mental clarity through Tai Chi or yoga? Do you light a candle for a loved one who has passed on? Do you post inspirational quotes on your bathroom mirror? Do you take 10 deep breaths upon rising in the morning? *Whatever you do that includes the focusing of your intention through a physical action is magical ritual.*

To become a powerful practitioner of magic, it is imperative to create a daily practice, done in solitude. Practicing with others is a joy, but it is always necessary to, first and foremost, continually cultivate a foundation of the self.

Depending on what's going on in my life, my rituals change. Yet, I have a core group of rituals that I practice on a fairly consistent basis. Some seasons, I focus my total energies on a single daily ritual in a very intense way: I am very adamant about doing that one thing every single day, no matter what. For example, I often have periods in my life where I perform the Japanese art of Reiki (hands-on healing/bodywork) every single day for half an hour for thirty consecutive days. In other seasons or in other years, I am like a honeybee, seeking out and enjoying a variety of flowers. The following is a list of my favorite solitary rituals. As you might notice, the list I have for solitary practice is longer than the list in the next section, which describes practice with others. This is to emphasize that a practice of the self is the firm (and only possible!) basis for building practice with others.

One must attain the discipline necessary to love, accept, and understand self. Without this, no joyful relationships can be possible.

These rituals have brought immense clarity and vision to my life. I encourage you to try some, and see if you notice a change in your perception of your own power.

- **Bowing at the Altar.** There is an altar in my bedroom. It is a special area, designed to evoke a sense of wonder, joy and awe. My altar is decorated with incense, flowers, shells, sand, crystals, feathers, pictures of my mentors, and other objects from nature. I come to my altar at night, before bed, and I bow before it, allowing gratefulness to fill my heart. Through the outward physical action of the bow, I display my inward humbleness and gratitude. I reflect on the beauty of the day that has passed, and I set an intention for my sleep to be deep and restorative. Bowing at the altar brings a lovely conclusion to my day, a moment where I remind myself that even though I am but a mere fragment of the Whole, I am a beautiful being that has tremendous power because I am connected, because I am unified with the Whole. By bowing, I show gratitude for my life, and set my intention to use this life in the service of spreading light throughout the world.

- **Day of Silence.** On a day of silence, I do not speak with others. I journey inward. By giving myself a break from the job of moving my consciousness outward (through verbal words, writing, and other forms of communication), I allow myself to relax and settle into myself. By the end of one of these days, I am noticeably more peaceful, and I find I can more easily tap into my intuition. However, it must be stated that on these days, there is always for me a moment or two where the temptation to break the silence is quite strong. Going through this temptation and coming out clean on the other side is usually a painful process. I find, however, that this pain is necessary. In a way, the pain is redemptive. For example, if I set the intention that undergoing this day of silence will help me conquer feelings of anger—perhaps sprouting from a relationship difficulty that is going on in my life at the time—then I will feel, during some moment during that day, that if I speak I will be relieved of the anger that is suddenly bubbling up inside of me. The temptation to speak seems overwhelming! However, *I must feel the anger fully*; I do not use communication to numb the pain that the anger has brought. I feel it fully within myself; I ride the wave of the emotion, without looking to analyze it or express it to/with another. I just feel it. After I resist the temptation to communicate, I usually have a spontaneous insight for why my anger has been manifesting. That insight brings me great relief, great joy.

- **Dream Journal.** Before sleep, I write a question in a notebook and put the notebook and pen beside my bed. I set the intention that the question will be answered. The question I ask is about a personal issue that has brought me great confusion—for whatever reason, I have not been able to clearly hear my voice of desire.

    Like clockwork, within a few days or a week, I have a dream that answers the question. I can then lean over in bed, grab the notebook and scribble down what I remember without even opening my eyes, and then easily fall back asleep. Sometimes the dream will hold the exact words about what I should do or think. For example, I once asked a question about what I should do to prepare myself for a weeklong silent retreat. Somewhere between sleeping and waking, the words came into my mind: "Appreciate everything you have." Those words helped me move into the week, with less fear and doubt.

Sometimes, the dream will be symbolic, and then interpretation is necessary. For example, I once asked whether I should move out of my current apartment because the rent was going up. I then dreamt the whole night about my hands and a massage table, swirling in a cloud, my body radiating orgasmically with feelings of abundance and pleasure. The dream was easy to interpret: My work would soon veer into the direction of sacred sexual healing, offering me the extra money I needed to stay in the apartment that I so loved.

It is important to do your own interpretation of your own dream symbols—don't leave it to Internet research or the numerous dream books you can purchase. As you journal your dreams over the course of months and years, you will begin to notice patterns, and understand what specific symbols mean for *you*. These symbols will not have the same meaning for anyone else. For example, I know when I dream of the singer-songwriter Leonard Cohen, my life is about to change drastically. For me, a Leonard Dream is partly a warning that I need to be aware that change is coming, but also it's a kind of blessing—because, inevitably, he will kiss me and whisper a wise message in my ear.

- **Intentional To Do List.** Power and clarity come when we can cut the clutter, slow down, and focus on the essentials. When I am feeling scattered, anxious, or overworked, I make a To Do list for the following day. Often, this list is short, including usually no more than four or five items. (For me, I normally want to move at a fast pace, so intending to do only a small number of things is a huge spiritual challenge for me!)

  The Intentional To Do List includes only those activities that will assist in your spiritual growth. For example, recently I made the list that on a Thursday I would only:

phone my Reiki client, perform a Reiki self-healing session, oil pull (an Ayurvedic detox treatment), sunbathe, and exercise. I also specified that after the call with my client, I would turn off all technologies for the rest of the day, as a method of manifesting a more reflective, slow-paced day. In sum, the act of writing down what I would do as well as what I would refrain from doing—and then actually carrying out that intention—is an extremely powerful form of magic. By having the courage to carry out what we intend (no more, no less) for a single day, we realize we have the power to fashion our *entire lives*, carving its moldable, flexible form into moments and activities that allow our consciousness to evolve, our hearts to open.

- **Prayer.** Every time I have sat at my desk to write another page of *Opening Love*, I have always begun with a few moments of prayer. I put my hands together in front of my heart, and, closing my eyes, I ask aloud that my fingers type only the words that will bring the highest benefit to those who read. Although many religions use prayer to request assistance from a specific deity, I simply ask "the universe." When you pray, please insert whatever word or phrase that feels comfortable for you: Source, Goddess, God, Cosmos, Love, Jesus, Shiva, Buddha, Krishna. The word you choose does not really matter. Focus your intention through the physical action of your spoken words and *mudra* (hand position), allowing your heart to open and connect to the eternal oneness that is your birthright.

∞

## Rituals: Magic with Others

Coming together with loved ones to practice magic is potent. The uplifting feeling one receives from collaborating with others through ritual is almost beyond words. Some of the most profound moments of my life have happened when I have come together with others to bring about an intention.

For example, I recently enlisted my loved ones, as well as acquaintances, in a long-term and incredibly powerful healing ritual. I changed my name. For many years—nearly my whole life in fact—I have struggled with chronic health problems. Knowing the power of words, I researched various names. I delighted to find "Anya," which means inexhaustibility in Sanskrit. (Among yoginis, magicians and other spiritual practitioners, the language of Sanskrit, one of the most ancient languages, is infamous for its magical properties.) As my various illnesses have caused a lack of vital energy, it was/is my intention to boost my life force through the use of this new name. Each time another mouth forms the word Anya, I feel a small zing—a subtle electrical charge of energy in my spine. Since the claiming of my new name, my sick days have decreased to the point where I no longer feel I can accurately call myself chronically ill. For the most part, I am a healthy person, with enough energy for not only myself, but also to share with others. I am indeed humbly grateful to anyone who calls me Anya, forsaking my old name. Without this assistance, my recovery might have taken much longer.

If your aim is to create magical relationships, you do not need to study under the tutelage of a shaman or guru. All you need is your own awesome body, the claiming of an intention in your mind, and the creative collaboration of loving intimates. The following are two rituals you can perform with a partner or multiple partners. You can set whatever specific intention fits that particular time, place and mood. You can set a simple intention, such as "We use this ritual to bond more deeply." Or, you can set an intention that seems more complex, specific, grand, or far-reaching, such as "Through our ritual today, allow love and light to dissolve the darkness of war between the Israelis and Palestinians." Open the love and think big, trusting that your ritual, no matter what it is, will benefit all beings.

- **Connection Day.** Use the Earth as your tool in this ritual. Disconnect from human-made technologies—leave your cell phones and laptops at home—and spend an entire day, from sunrise to sunset, outside in the open air, near trees or water. Spend this day with one, two, or more people whom you love. Find a park, beach, sand dune, forest, hiking trail—anything outdoors works. At the beginning of the day, hold the hand(s) of your loved one(s), and speak out loud, in unison, your intention. For instance, your intention could be: "we manifest a carefree, silly attitude today." Or: "we dissolve the anger between us, shifting into peace and love." Intend whatever is needed at that time. Your Connection Day, no matter what intention you set, will have the result of connecting you with your loved one(s), as well as connecting you to the natural world. As you are out in the sun and air, feel your anxiety melt away. This is not the time to plan for the future or dwell on the past. *Remain glued to the present moment by engaging all your senses.* At the end of this luminous day, take a moment to close the ritual by saying thanks to yourselves for taking the time for this ritual. Reflect and feel gratitude.
- **Planting a Seed.** Gather your loved one(s) near you, and discuss what you would like to manifest in the future. Does your relationship need more empathy? More gentleness? Better communication? More spontaneity? Forgiveness? How is the relationship now, and how would you like it to be in the future? What added element would increase the joy of the relationship? After discussing, obtain a seed and prepare some soil. Each person holds the seed for a few moments, closing their eyes, and visualizing

the intention being put into the seed. Once the seed has absorbed the energy of the intention, plant the seed. Plant it in a space you will see every day. As you watch the seed grow, take the time, as often as you can, to slow down to gaze at the plant, appreciating its beauty, its strength, its unique characteristics. Be on the watch for your intention unfolding in the material realm. The plant will be a reminder; the plant will be your helper.

## Challenges and Possibilities

Relationships are not easy. Long-term ones can be especially challenging. You will often find that your partners and close intimates are the ones who challenge you in ways that shake you to your very foundation. Your core shakes, and you sometimes even find yourself wondering if you will literally die from conflict or change. Sometimes you may even find yourself doubting whether you really love the ones you've loved for many years. These times of confusion can, and often do, manifest as physical pain in the heart or as a blocked-up feeling in the throat. Being in a relationship is not easy. In fact, it will be the biggest challenge of your life.

You are, now, on a path of rapid evolution. Can you feel it? You are increasingly able to see the needless division, hatred, and fear that separate most of the world. You are in the process of intentionally releasing the normative conditioning; you are living with courage and compassion in your everyday intimate relationships, knowing that although your choices will not be lauded by mainstream society, you are doing what you know, deep in your bones, that you *must* do. There is simply no other way now.

And there is so much awe and beauty to behold! To gaze into the eyes of your beloveds is to gaze into the eyes of divinity itself—"divinity" not as some abstract concept, but as a living and breathing reality. Divinity is the energy of love—pure love, without limits. It is free, fathomless, and ineffable. The words in this book cannot describe it.

When you look carefully, you realize you are one specific form that has emerged from the All That Is. This shape you have now, this name, this life narrative: this is one star, this is one beacon of light in a cosmos of infinity. And you celebrate, because you know death does not end you. Death is merely a transition: an adoption of new form.

You, dear star, have taken this form in this particular lifetime to enjoy, to experience, to learn, to forgive, and to love. You have forgotten that you intentionally took this form, yet you are increasingly coming to feel, usually against all rational logic, that you have a mission here. You have a purpose. Your life is magnificently important. And there is no god of judgment up in the clouds that is separate from you that you must worship or obey or fear — that corrupted, outdated concept of "God" is, thankfully, passing away from collective human consciousness. What is replacing that outdated concept is the *experience* of something deeper. Something exhilarating.

As your consciousness expands, reaching new levels of awareness, you begin to love yourself and you begin to love your lovers, friends, family and even strangers on the street because you recognize in them the same thread of divinity that runs through your own heart. You treat them with compassion, as you would like to be treated. You recognize their inherent freedom, because you yourself are inherently free. This is a free-will universe.

You are on what some might call the path of the mystic. You are a warrior, fighting a peaceful battle against the normal. You bring light to illuminate darkness. You do not fear being called crazy or naïve, because you know those judgments are based on outdated ways of thinking, ways of thinking that do not take into account the unity of all beings and the possibilities of the human being. You do not mind what others think. *You know what you know*, and it's beyond logic. The voice of desire is your teacher.

You will be challenged. You will endure difficult times. Sexual and romantic relationships continue to be the single most cause of stress for people, and set the conditions for heartache, ego-gratification, selfish desires, and negative fears and worries. This is why so many religions suggest a celibate path for people who are serious about pursuing a spiritual life. Negotiating and growing in relationships while simultaneously evolving spiritual awareness is an incredible feat, an incredible trial. Most people, in the history of the planet, haven't been able to do it.

You will be able to do it. This book is a torch, a model, a hope for you. The planet is changing. There is a frequency shift happening, and this book is not the only testament. Through opening yourself to the challenges of loving relationships, you blast yourself forward... you rapidly progress to a higher dimension of understanding, a level where problems of jealousy and insecurity are just a memory.

## No Conclusion

There is no conclusion to this book. For as the Buddha taught: there are no beginnings, no endings, no comings, no goings, no birth, and no death. The way the universe works is pure eternal being-ness. There is no separation; there are no goodbyes.

We have the power, already, to manifest the kind of life, the kind of relationships we want. If we listen to desire and if we cultivate the courage necessary to discipline ourselves to go against the tides of the normal, then we will find ourselves living a life of joy, both in the moments we spend alone in peaceful and accepting solitude, as well as the moments we spend with other lovely beings.

As our consciousness brightens, the darkness of what we have been taught as children will begin to fade. Intentional relation-ships will naturally evolve, forming the tapestry for our daily lives. Magic will infuse how we perceive and interact with the Earth and with the social world. Our faces and fingertips will radiate light. That light will draw others, who have similar missions.

We will tune our frequencies together. We will change everything.

# An Invitation to Know What Only You Know

April opens out of what may appear to be nothing
—blasts sent as beams transmuted into blossoms.
> About the everything in nothing, the love in fear,
> the *yes* in the *no* of winter and otherwise, ask The
> Moon. She knows because she's always present.

And July pumpkins tucked just underground with
the intention to grow, the purpose of living. Why?
> Why live in relationship with other beings?
> Why eat seeds? Why make love?
> As above, so below: Look to the rising-setting Sun.

Please do not take the author's word for it. Go out,
into October, and Octobers next and next, and be
your ever-present, conscious Self. Myth as a
quest of ego, has scarred you like a jack-o-lantern.
> You're not alone in this either, and you're still you.

You are still and always love and light, sent from above,
to look within and uncover the truth, sometimes sought
on January's 1st day. Conception brought forth by this
> poem or this book or any reference is the beginning. It
> is the call inviting you to transform through alignment
> > with that which only you know.

*Andrew Trahan*
*October 2014*
*Boulder, Colorado*

# References

### Prelude

1. Osho, *Courage: The Joy of Living Dangerously* (New York, NY: St. Martin's Griffin, 1999), p. 119

### Introduction

2. bell hooks, *All About Love: New Visions* (New York, NY: Harper Perennial, 2000), p. 14

3. Kathy Labriola, *Love in Abundance: A Counselor's Advice on Open Relationships* (Eugene, OR: Greenery Press, 2010), p. 4

4. Deborah Anapol, *Polyamory in the Twenty-First Century: Love and Intimacy with Multiple Partners* (Lanham, MD: Rowman & Littlefield Publishers, Inc., 2010), p. 4

5. BF Malle et al., *Intentions and Intentionality: Foundations of Social Cognition* (Cambridge, MA: MIT Press, 2001)

6. Wayne W. Dyer, *The Power of Intention* (Carlsbad, CA: Hay House, Inc., 2010), p. 7

7. Lynne McTaggart, *The Intention Experiment* (New York, NY: Atria Paperback, 2007), p. xxi

8. Brené Brown, *Daring Greatly* (New York: Gotham Books, 2012)

9. M. Scott Peck, *The Road Less Travelled* (New York: Simon & Schuster, 1978)

10. Joan Gattuso, *A Course in Love: Powerful Teachings on Love, Sex, and Personal Fulfillment* (New York: HarperCollins, 1996), p. 86

11. Paul Tillich, *The Courage to Be* (New Haven and London: Yale University Press, 1952), p. 29

12. Meg Barker, *Rewriting the Rules: An Integrative Guide to Love, Sex and Relationships* (London: Routledge, 2013), p. 7

13. Eckhart Tolle, *A New Earth* (New York: Penguin Group, 2005)

14. Gangaji, *The Diamond in Your Pocket: Discovering Your True*

*Radiance* (Boulder, CO: Sounds True, Inc., 2007), p. 10

## Chapter 1: Dust and Dissatisfaction

15. Eckhart Tolle, *A New Earth* (New York: Penguin Group, 2005), p. 14
16. Michael Warner, *The Trouble with Normal: Sex, Politics, and the Ethics of Queer Life* (Cambridge, MA: Harvard University Press, 1999)
17. bell hooks, *All About Love: New Visions* (New York, NY: Harper Perennial, 2000), p. 48
18. bell hooks, *All About Love: New Visions* (New York, NY: Harper Perennial, 2000), p. 48
19. Eve Kosofsky Sedgwick, *Tendencies* (Duke University Press, 1993), p. 6
20. William J. Doherty, *The Intentional Family: How to Build Family Ties in Our Modern World* (Addison-Wesley Publishing Company, Inc., 1997)
21. Meg Barker, *Rewriting the Rules: An Integrative Guide to Love, Sex and Relationships* (London and New York: Routledge, 2013), p. 2

## Chapter 2: Queering Desire

22. Lao Tzu, *Tao Te Ching* (Fall River Press, 2005), p. 83
23. Don Miguel Ruiz, *The Four Agreements* (San Rafael, CA: Amber-Allen Publishing, 1997)
24. Osho, *Courage: The Joy of Living Dangerously* (New York, NY: St. Martin's Griffin, 1999), p. 55
25. Gospel of Thomas, Verse 70
26. Osho, *Courage: The Joy of Living Dangerously* (New York, NY: St. Martin's Griffin, 1999), pp. 1–2

## Chapter 3: Beyond Orientation

27. Osho, *Courage: The Joy of Living Dangerously* (New York, NY: St. Martin's Griffin, 1999), p. x

28. Eckhart Tolle, *The Power of Now: A Guide to Spiritual Enlightenment* (Vancouver: Namaste Publishing, 1999), p. 15

29. Maria Pallotta-Chiarolli, *Border Sexualities, Border Families in Schools* (Lanham: Rowman and Littlefield Publishers, Inc., 2010), p. 33

30. Deborah Anapol, *Polyamory in the Twenty-First Century: Love and Intimacy with Multiple Partners* (Lanham, MD: Rowman & Littlefield Publishers, Inc., 2010), p. 4

31. Karen Armstrong, *The Spiral Staircase: My Climb Out of Darkness* (New York: Anchor Books, 2004), p. 268

32. Sara Ahmed, *Queer Phenomenology: Orientation, Objects, Others* (Durham and London: Duke University Press, 2006), p. 85

33. Sara Ahmed, *Queer Phenomenology: Orientation, Objects, Others* (Durham and London: Duke University Press, 2006), p. 68

34. Joan Gattuso, *A Course in Love: Powerful Teachings on Love, Sex, and Personal Fulfillment* (New York: HarperCollins, 1996), pp. 33–34

## Chapter 4: Beyond Jealousy

35. Alice Walker, *Absolute Trust in the Goodness of the Earth: New Poems* (New York: Random House, 2003), p. 34

36. Mystic Life, *Spiritual Polyamory* (Lincoln, NE: iUniverse, Inc., 2004), p. 3

37. Barbara Carrellas, *Urban Tantra: Sacred Sex for the Twenty-First Century* (New York: Celestial Arts, 2007)

38. Caroline Myss, *Why People Don't Heal and How They Can* (New York, NY: Three Rivers Press, 1997), pp. 62–63

39. William Carlos Williams, *The Collected Poems of William Carlos Williams, Volume II* (New York: New Directions Books, 1986), p. 141

40. Dossie Easton and Janet W. Hardy, *The Ethical Slut: A Practical Guide to Polyamory, Open Relationships & Other*

*Adventures* (New York: Celestial Arts, 2009), pp. 56–57

41. Osho, *Courage: The Joy of Living Dangerously* (New York: St. Martin's Griffin, 1999), p. 64

42. Parker J. Palmer, *A Hidden Wholeness: The Journey Toward an Undivided Life* (San Francisco, CA: Jossey-Bass, 2004), p. 5

## Chapter 5: New Energy Investments

43. Eckhart Tolle, *The Power of Now: A Guide to Spiritual Enlightenment* (Vancouver: Namaste Publishing, 1999), p. 42

44. Parker J. Palmer, *A Hidden Wholeness: The Journey Toward an Undivided Life* (San Francisco, CA: Jossey-Bass, 2004), p. 22

45. Deborah M. Anapol, *Polyamory: The New Love Without Limits: Secrets of Sustainable Intimate Relationships* (San Rafael, CA: Intinet Resource Center, 1997), p. 95

46. Gangaji, *The Diamond in Your Pocket: Discovering Your True Radiance* (Boulder, CO: Sounds True, Inc., 2005), p. 26

## Chapter 6: Healing and Forgiveness

47. Stephen Russell, *Barefoot Doctor's Guide to the Tao: A Spiritual Handbook for the Urban Warrior* (New York: Times Books, 1998), p. 185

48. Joan Gattuso, *A Course in Love: Powerful Teachings on Love, Sex, and Personal Fulfillment* (New York: HarperCollins, 1996), p. 126

49. Caroline Myss, *Why People Don't Heal and How They Can* (New York, NY: Three Rivers Press, 1997), p. 18

50. Thich Nhat Hanh, *The Art of Power* (New York: HarperCollins Publishers, 2007), p. 33

## Chapter 7: Magical Relationships

51. Don Miguel Ruiz, *The Four Agreements* (San Rafael, CA: Amber-Allen Publishing, 1997)

52. Stephen Russell, *Barefoot Doctor's Guide to the Tao: A Spiritual Handbook for the Urban Warrior* (New York: Times Books,

1998), p. 74

53. Starhawk, *The Spiral Dance: A Rebirth of the Ancient Religion of the Great Goddess* (New York: HarperSanFrancisco, 1989), p. 10

54. Don Miguel Ruiz, *The Four Agreements* (San Rafael, CA: Amber-Allen Publishing, 1997), pp. 123–124

CHANGE
MAKERS
BOOKS

Changemakers publishes books for individuals committed to transforming their lives and transforming the world. Our readers seek to become positive, powerful agents of change. Changemakers books inform, inspire, and provide practical wisdom and skills to empower us to create the next chapter of humanity's future.
Please visit our website at www.changemakers-books.com